# Your 2 Minds

*Using Your Mind to Transform Your Life*

*Written by*

*Suzana Mihajlovic*

*This book is dedicated to my late Baba Nada (grandma Nada). By letting your own light shine, you allowed everyone who came into contact with you to shine. I love you to eternity.*

*"Every living being is an engine to the wheel work of the universe. Though seemingly affected only by its immediate surrounding, the sphere of external influence extends to infinite distance." - Nikola Tesla*

# Table of Contents

# Your2Minds Endorsements

*"Change happens from the inside out – it starts in your mind and it starts with you. Suzana's inspirational stories and common sense approach to making quantum leaps in your results make this book a guide for growth and improvement. Apply the principles and change your life. You won't ever look back."*

— Bob Proctor, Master Success Coach

*"What if I told you that this book could remove whatever obstacles you may be facing and could create a huge, yet positive, shift in your life? Purpose is a driving force behind who you are and what you do. Suzana has learned that simple truth through her own compelling experiences that she shares within the pages of this heartfelt and inspirational book. She will help guide you to discovering your purpose by teaching you some simple tools and techniques that you can apply to your own life. A must read for anyone wanting to change their life by changing their mindset."*

— Peggy McColl, New York Times Best Selling Author

*I absolutely loved reading Your2Minds by Suzana Mihajlovic! If you think this book is about the conscious and sub-conscious minds...hang on, because there's a delicious twist! This book opened up my mind and heart to new possibilities that I hadn't even considered. Devour this book and enjoy the brilliant insights. Suzana Mihajlovic is a genius!*

— Brett Sampson, President, Sampson Consulting

*Your2Minds will make you have a deeper perspective on what goes on inside your head. It will force you to reflect on what you have done, look at what you are doing and have a vision for your future. Suzana gets you to write down your thoughts and answers to her questions forcing you to engage the mind at a deeper level and tell your subconscious mind that you are ready to make a change and take action. The exercises help you to connect, identify, and recognize what you need to do.*

*She shares her personal experience showing us how one must choose the path and want to change. We will have different voices trying to direct us. No one is exempt from having 2Minds but we must make the choice of which we allow to be the dominant mind and use it to transform our lives. "*

— Makini Smith, Author of A Walk in My Stilettos

*In this inspiring, open-hearted, easy to follow book, Suzana engages us with her personal life experiences and strategies that have transformed her life. Through this book, she shares those insights and provides useful, practical exercises to challenge her readers to work towards their full potential.*

— Dr. Reenu Farrugia, Psy.D

Your2Minds is a book you will devour. One to keep close at hand and to read and re-read.

If you absorb and implement the ideas and strategies that Suzana suggests your life and results will change beyond all recognition.

Karen Mullins Consulting, Principal, Karen Mullins Consulting

This book will undoubtedly change the way you see, feel and deal with your mind and life. Discover your inner power now!

— Sheila Benton, Personal and Business Consultant

*Your2Minds is written like a conversation between you and a trusted friend. Suzana shows you how to draw more meaning, greater satisfaction, and profound purpose from your own life with knowledge that comes from a deep place of wisdom. A conversation that could prove to be a turning point to building your life in ways you barely dare dream about.*

— Monte Young, USAF Major (ret), Southwest Airlines Pilot

# My Gratitude

I have so much to be grateful for, not only in making this book a reality but also in my life in general. I am lucky. Many people enrich my life, make it more joyful, fuller, and brighter. Although I cannot mention every single one of them here, my gratitude goes out to them all just the same.

Before I begin to acknowledge the people in my life, I would like to acknowledge the thing that made the most difference in my finally stepping out and finishing the book I attempted to write so many times: *Thinking Into Results*. This program turned things around for me and so many of my clients. Thank you, Bob Proctor and Sandy Gallagher, for your brilliance in putting this program together. I am proud to be a Proctor Gallagher Institute Consultant.

One incredible woman has transformed this book to make it have the impact I always intended it to and she deserves to be the first person acknowledged I this book, and that is my brilliant editor, Vesna Zuban, from Uptown Words Editing and Writing Services, your skills are second to none. You are truly phenomenal at your art. Thank you. I am so proud of you and what you have accomplished since doing the Thinking Into Results program.

Peggy McColl, your belief in me to get the job done assisted me in opening my mind to allow my heart to speak the words that are in this book. You took me in and having you by my side helped me finally accomplish my mission, my dream. My goal to write a book has been living inside me for forty years, and without your guidance, it would probably still be only a dream that I would accomplish 'one day'. The importance of having a coach or mentor was proof in your dedication to my mission. Thank you.

I would like to thank my loving family. You have all stood by me through thick and thin, through celebration and proud moments, as well as through my darkest periods and embarrassing falls. You deserve the first acknowledgement because of your unconditional love and support and all that you have guided me through and taught me. You have always been there and loved me even during the times that it was painful to be around me. Thank you.

I would like to acknowledge and thank my incredible partner. You have been my greatest support in writing this book. Your honesty and frankness always push me to be better and do better, to dig deeper into my potential and keep drawing out greater quality. Your support and belief in me never go unappreciated. You continue to inspire me every day by being the person you are. Thank you.

To my nephews and niece — Stefan, Luka, and Sara. You bring joy to my heart and light to my world every day with just a thought. You are the lights of my life. Never allow your own deep inner light to dim. You are perfect in your own imperfection and never forgot you could accomplish anything you ever dreamed of if you were ready to keep working on your mind. I am so blessed and grateful to have you. Although you are no longer little, you are still Teta Suzy's bundles of joy.

To my dear friend Reen. Your support of me and belief in me never cease to fail. I must be the luckiest person in the world to have such a dedicated friend that I find in you. I am blessed. Thank you.

To my Godchildren — Milica, Milena, Marcus, and Ellie. Thank you for choosing me for your 'Kuma.' Words cannot say how much love and light you bring to my heart. Keep focused on where you are going because if your Kuma could do it, so can you. Thank you.

To the children in my life — Cassandra, Nicholas, Zalaika, Jaidan, Jordan, Connor, Mihail, Ava, Mila, Luka, Milan, Natalija, Arianna, and Nick. Thank you for all that you contribute to me and the world. You are my pure joy. Teta Suzy, or Kuma Suzy for some of you, believes in you, and I cannot wait to witness your beautiful achievements in life. Remember never to let your light be dimmed. Thank you.

To my dear friends and relatives, who are too large in number to mention here, but as a start, Marina, Vicky, Mirjana, Tanja, Sofija, Vesna, Suzana, Sonja, Draga, Danijela, Toula, Irene, Biljana, Luciana, Sue, Suri, Monica, thank you for sticking by me throughout the years, for your ongoing support and loyalty. Thank you for making my life so much more fulfilling. Thank you to my big cousin Olivera, I miss you but continue to be inspired by you, Sladja and Marina, always in my heart.

# Foreword

Purpose is a driving force behind who you are and what you do. Suzana has learned that simple truth through her own compelling experiences that she shares within the pages of this heartfelt and inspirational book. She will help guide you to discovering your purpose by offering you some simple tools and techniques that you can apply to your own life.

If you are yet to discover your purpose, there may be some lingering questions that are often in the back of your mind. For example:

What is my purpose?

Am I truly happy?

Who do I want to be?

Am I living the life of my dreams?

What if I told you that this book could remove whatever obstacles you may be facing and create a huge, yet positive, shift in your life?

I have been in the personal development business for many years and have spent many of those years learning about why we do the things we do, and why we don't do many of the things we are capable of doing. Many people are aware that their lives are not all that they had hoped for and would like to change that, but very few are aware that we are set up for success by nature — we are all created with infinite potential.

I feel honored to be invited to write the foreword for this book. Suzana became a client of mine, and from the moment I met her, I knew she had the power to change people's lives. When we met she asked me, with tears in her eyes, if there was any way possible that she could write her book in seven days; my answer was a resounding "yes!" In those few minutes I spoke with her, I felt her passion for transforming the world and saw her enthusiasm as she talked about her big dream of sharing what she had learned.

Suzana learned from the best, Bob Proctor, when she decided to become a Proctor Gallagher Institute (PGI) Consultant. The training taught her how to assist people with goals and shifting paradigms so they can have the success in life that they had always dreamed of having.

This book will enlighten you to discover your own path. Suzana has created an easy to use guideline for choosing goals that will improve your life, both now and in the future, and goals that fall in line with the person you are and want to be.

Success and happiness do not happen by accident. People create their own lasting happiness and success by creating positive habits, being disciplined, and choosing their thoughts and actions.

"All you need is the plan, the road map, and the courage to press on to your destination."
~ Earl Nightingale

There are many excuses that we tell ourselves that prevent us from being truly happy, and within these pages, you will learn how to move past them. Not only is the content incredible and highly actionable, but the exercises and thought-provoking questions at the end of each chapter will force you to dig deeper and make the positive change you desire.

Since we are on a constant quest to better ourselves and our lives, *Your-2Minds* empowers you to do what you must to be your best you. The key is not to dwell on the past but rather take those lessons and apply them to your life today. Embrace your failures as experiences and use them to motivate yourself to do better in the future.

Use this book as your road map to make changes in your life that you never thought were possible: the extraordinary power lies within YOU!

Peggy McColl
New York Times Best Selling Author

# Preface — A Message of Gratitude to My Mentor Bob Proctor

*"Without you the Universe would be out of alignment."*

*"I am a spiritual person living in a human body, not a human body with a spirit." - Bob Proctor*

In order to succeed in life, every person needs a mentor. I am about to share with you an experience that I had with my mentor. This experience shifted my life in a profound way, and I would like you to open up your consciousness so that you too can have your own life-altering experience. When you truly open yourself up to the meaning of this, I hope that you will notice a shift in your thinking about who you are, your life, and life in general.

Toronto, September 2017: I was sitting in a room full of people, and my mentor, Bob Proctor, said this:

*"Did you know that nothing in this entire Universe would move in the precise order it moves in your absence? Did you know that if you weren't here, the Universe would literally be out of alignment?"*

xvii

There is something remarkable about this man. He is one of those rare people who literally practices what he preaches. Just having him in a room lifts the entire vibration, and when he says something, you feel it resonate in every cell of your being.

When Bob spoke those compelling words, my body reacted. I felt them and Bob's energy at the very depth of my core. Making this immensely profound statement about who I was allowed my energy to lift to a level where Spirit was able to enter and do its work through and within me. I have been around so many amazing people, but never has anything in my life resonated as loudly as this.

Bob lives on an epically high vibration of love and a deep, unquestioning, inner knowing of and belief in the principles he teaches. I do not doubt that the one hundred and fifty or so people in that room also felt something shift inside them. The vibration was strong. One man in a room, with so many people, created a shift by lifting every single person there to the level of his own vibration.

This was enough proof for me, and all those who experienced it, that a single person can change the world by changing themselves first. Bob learned about his infinite greatness and changed his mindset and subconscious paradigms in his late twenties and, as a result, went from being in debt to a millionaire, within a very short period of time.

As remarkable a person as Bob is, he alone could not have transformed my thinking and uplifted my vibration. I chose to open up and learn about who I was and what I could do to change my mindset, so that I too could experience more of my infinite potential. I was ready, I was willing, and I had wanted change for a long time. I had been working on the spiritual practice of "Letting Go and Letting God" for quite a few months before that experience. I craved that strong spiritual connection with Source for most of my life and had experienced it many times. I worked hard on changing my deeply embedded mindset and subconscious paradigms that had not been benefiting me. This time, sitting about one meter away from Bob and hearing his words, I felt as though I needed to allow myself to be guided on to the next step. I wanted so much more for myself and my life. I yearned to dig deeper and to unfold that infinite well of internal greatness. I prayed almost every day for guidance, and that day, I knew my prayers were being answered.

Let me explain what Bob's words meant to me and why they affected me so strongly. Most of us tend to undermine ourselves and our capabilities to such a small and insignificant level that we only ever use a fraction of our actual potential. We often let fear and the negative messages we carry in our mind control us and make decisions for us. We blindly accept that we are not smart enough, not good enough, not beautiful enough, not worthy enough, or simply not enough. We also tend to allow others to feed us these falsehoods. However, what we have missed is that the Universe is an infinite, immensely and profoundly loving, powerful, and creative force. And we are a part of that creation! The Universe created us. It wanted us and created every one of us as an intricate and irreplaceable part of itself through its omnipotent and everlasting love for us. So, if we are a part of that creation, our presence is critical, in the bigger scheme of things, for the Universe to continue functioning as a complete whole. Take one element out of the Universe, and it ceases to function in its natural alignment. Therefore, if we took *you* out of the Universe, the Universe would be out of alignment. Do you get it? If not, please go back and read that again.

Now, if something hasn't moved inside you, I have not explained this properly, or you have not yet fully grasped what this says about your magnificence.

The above is my story, which I am drawn to share with you. But this book is for you and about you. So please, sit quietly for a few minutes, close your eyes, and say to yourself:

*"Did you know if you weren't here, the Universe would literally be out of alignment?"*

Say it as many times as you need to until it sinks in. No matter what you have experienced, or the doubts that keep coming up, this is the truth. Now, I would like you to put your name in front of that statement:

*"... (Your name), did you know if you weren't here, the Universe would literally be out of alignment?"*

Now say it in front of your mirror. Write this statement down and put it in a place where you will see it every day and often. Carry it with you because once you truly experience the truth of this statement, your life will never be the same. Let it resonate. Do not read past this point until you feel it has resonated deep within you. Spend a day re-affirming this statement then come back to this book and read through it. There is nothing more important than you realizing this - not even finishing this book. It is the secret of how extraordinary you truly are. It is time to start changing your mindset so that you truly come to know your own worth, beauty and power. When your mindset changes, and you understand and believe this truth, your life will change to match it.

# PART 1:

## Extraordinary Living Through Your2minds

# Introduction

**Picture this scene.**

You're sitting at home one day when you decide to head out on your daily walk along the beach, but as you try to move off the sofa, you notice your body is not responding. It feels fatigued and heavy. How strange. You've been fit and agile for many years and haven't felt this kind of heaviness before. You try to get up off the sofa again, but the heaviness in your body continues to weigh you down. Bewildered, you try to hoist yourself up for the third time. Again, your body refuses to cooperate, so you decide to lie down on the sofa for a while. As you're lying there perplexed, you try to relax by mentally scanning your body and contracting and releasing each muscle. Relaxation exercises have always worked for you in the past. You try to move your legs, but it takes effort as they're aching and sluggish—just yesterday they were fine. You hear your bones crack as you slowly start to move your feet first. You then focus on moving your legs again, and although they're aching, you manage, but it takes twice as long as usual.

From where you're sitting, you can see out through your favorite art deco window — one of the features that compelled you to purchase your home many years ago. You love to sit by that window, watching the world go by, drinking your coffee and reading your favorite authors.

3

There's not a cloud in the sky outside and you yearn for the salty sea air, walking with the pebbled, wet sand beneath your bare feet, listening to the sound of waves gently crashing onto the shore. You always dreamed of a beach lifestyle, and this beautiful art deco home with the round window two blocks away from it was your ideal sanctuary. The water soothes you. It calms your mind and nourishes your soul. But today, for some reason, you can't reach it.

As you bend down to rub your aching legs, your hands take you by surprise. They're wrinkled with spots you've never noticed before — the hands of an elderly person. You're perplexed and start to panic. What's happening? Something is not right.

With great effort, you finally manage to rise off the sofa, your legs shaky and weak, but you're determined to move. You feel as if you're in someone else's body as you slowly start moving towards the bathroom. The reflection in the mirror frightens and confuses you. You shriek, *"What's happened to me?"* Staring back at you is the face of an elderly person with gray hair, hallowed eyes and wrinkled skin. You don't want to believe that it is you, but you know it is. The eyes give it away. They are your eyes; same color, same shape, same expression. The only thing missing in them is that youthful spark that you once had.

Your once thick, shiny hair has thinned and is now completely gray, and your once plump, rosy cheeks are gaunt and sagging. As you stare at the mirror in shock, your entire life starts to flash before you.

Suddenly, with a gasp of air, you wake up sweating, disoriented, and shaking. What just happened? You must have been dreaming, yet it all felt so real, and you know it was your reflection in that mirror. You lie there in bed, unable to move, not wanting to get up. The 'dream' has shaken you to the core. It takes you a few moments to compose yourself.

As you lie there reflecting on what you just experienced, you realize that the reflection in the mirror was the you of your future- in your final days.

The dream has a profound impact on you. Seeing yourself in that state and watching your life flash before you brings home the reality that your life *is* flashing by right now. It highlighted the areas of your life where you have been fearful, where you have doubted yourself, and where you have prevented yourself from going the extra mile in creating the life that your heart so desired. It made you recognize how much time you have wasted carrying the burdens of your past; it helped you understand all the resentment and anger toward others that has been weighing you down like a ton of bricks. It explained why you have had so many blocks in your life, and why things didn't work out for you. But, more than anything, it forced you to confront the reality that it was you holding yourself back and nobody else. This was all contrary to what you had thought before. Often you would blame others for your situation, and when you couldn't blame another, you would blame circumstance.

Most importantly, this dream made you understand that all those burdens and blocks were a waste of precious time because they didn't serve you; you now know that you have the choice to live your life differently from this moment forward. After this experience, you can never take your life for granted again.

$$\S \, \S \, \S$$

Hopefully this imaginary scenario has served its intended purpose, which is to highlight how crucial it is to make use of the time we have in this life. Whether we choose to live the way we truly want to or choose to become victims of our experiences, circumstances and others around us, the time will pass anyway. Wouldn't it be better to choose the happier, more fulfilled path?

One day we will all look in the mirror, and the image reflected at us will not be the image that we see today. If we are fortunate enough to reach old age and all that comes with it— gray hair, wrinkled skin and aching bones— we will see ourselves in one of two ways. Some will look back at their lives with contentment, pride, and satisfaction, while others will stare into a face full of regrets, dreams unrealized, and goals unfulfilled.

In my experience from speaking with people who have reached a ripe old age of 80 years and beyond, the thing they all seemed to echo was that life passes us by in a flash, so we should just relax and live it as fully and completely as we can, while we can. Common pearls of wisdom included, *"Don't worry too much what others think"*, *"Don't worry about what you should or shouldn't do"* and *"Take risks because what is life without risks?"*

Maybe life will not pass by as quickly as it did in that dream, but the days will pass. I've noticed this myself. When I was in my twenties, I would often hear people say: *"Enjoy it now because life speeds up once you hit your thirties and forties."* In some ways, I agree with this. However, I also find that we are conditioned to believe that life inevitably gets harder, or less enjoyable, as we age. I refuse to believe this, so my personal advice would be to approach each day with gratitude for the privilege of seeing it— of being alive. Your life can be as great as you want it to be, irrespective of your age. *Allow* yourself to live fully and joyously, and it will be so.

You see, we need to live with the attitude, or mindset, that although life can be painful, scary, and heartbreaking, it can also be precious and wondrous, if we choose to believe it can be.

The moral of this story is that life will go by no matter what. That is an obvious fact. And whether life goes by fast or slow doesn't really matter because there will come a day for each of us when we will look in the mirror for the last time. We don't like to think about this, but in order to live our best life today, we need to fully grasp this stark reality.

So, here is the question: When you look in the mirror that one last time, and you reflect back on the precious life that you have lived, what will your memories of your life reveal to you? Will you be proud and happy that you lived your best life? Or, will you be full of regrets and wishes that you didn't live it differently? Will you have taken risks and worked toward fulfilling your potential, or will you have created a life of misery, resentment, and fear? Will you have done the things that you dreamed of doing even though you were afraid? Did you make a difference to others? Did you follow your true passions?

### What will you think looking back on your life, as it is today?

This book has been written for the most important person on the planet— YOU! Although I have included stories and examples from my life, I truly hope that they resonate with you. I hope that they trigger something inside you that inspires a shift in your mindset, so that your mind can work for you and lead you toward the path that will make your heart and soul sing. At the end of your life, you can look back and say:

"…(your name), I love you! Thank you for being brave enough to give me all those fun and magnificent memories. Thank you for being strong enough to be you and for being wise enough to know that being YOU was enough. Thank you for taking risks, for getting up again when you fell so many times. Thank you for allowing me to grieve when I needed to grieve, to feel my emotions without suppressing them, to be who I truly am and to show up as the *magnificent, imperfect me. Thank you for the adventures, for the times that you stretched yourself and the growing and learning you were brave enough to do. Thank you for the extraordinary life that you have given me. Because of the decisions you have made in life, I have left a legacy for my loved ones and for all who have come to know me. Thank you for being courageous enough to allow me to do that. And thank you for living my life to the fullest through thick and thin!"*

In this book, we will explore the concept of Your2Minds in different scenarios and open up the journey of becoming more aware of who you truly are. We will explore ideas that will help you stop the thought patterns and paradigms that prevent you from living the extraordinary life that you deserve and were born to live. Before we begin, I would like to ask — are you brave enough to embark on this journey? I believe you are. Let's do this!

# Your Extraordinary Life Exercise

*"Follow your bliss and the Universe will open doors where there were only walls." - Joseph Campbell*

I suggest that you buy a Your2Minds journal. We will be doing a number of different exercises throughout this book which are deeply personal and will assist you to start changing your mindset, so that you can live your best life. Remember— this is it! You don't get another chance, so make up your mind to live your one life fully and authentically TODAY. That means doing the work, taking the time to invest in yourself, and confronting the fear or any other emotion that may be holding you back. Make sure you do the exercises. Once you have completed this book and the exercises in it, keep your journal because you will need to go back and reflect.

Before you continue reading, please take the time to complete the exercise in this chapter. Although most of us don't like to think about it, one of the most powerful things that you can do for yourself is to imagine what it will be like for you at the end of your life. By accepting that we only have limited time on this plane of existence, we will appreciate it more, with an increased willingness to do whatever it takes to make it great.

A lot of the spiritual teachers say that you can only live a great life by fully realizing that you will be gone one day. By thinking about life from that

9

perspective, it allows us to start appreciating every single day and every experience we have, whatever that experience may be. Upon discovering that he was close to death, Steve Jobs made the following statement:

*"Your time is limited, so don't waste it living someone else's life. Don't be trapped by dogma - which is living with the results of other people's thinking. Don't let the noise of others' opinions drown out your own inner voice. And most important, have the courage to follow your heart and intuition." -* Steve Jobs

For this exercise, I would like you to imagine yourself looking back into that mirror, years from now. Imagine that you are able to see images of your life flashing before you in your mind. Reflecting back on what you see, go through two scenarios:

## Scenario One

In the first scenario, imagine that your life went along on its current trajectory. Be honest with yourself and create a clear image in your mind. Once you have that clear image of where your life would likely be if you continued doing what you're doing now, write out the answers to the following questions:

| Question | Answer |
|---|---|
| What type of experiences and memories have you had? | |
| What regret/s do you have? | |
| Out of all of your regrets, which is the biggest or most significant? | |
| Why haven't you done or achieved the thing you would have really liked to in your life? | |

| Question | Answer |
|---|---|
| What would you change if you could? | |
| What decisions were you afraid to make that you wished you had? | |
| If you had made those decisions, what would your life have been like?<br><br>What experiences would you have had? | |
| What grievances and resentments have you carried? | |
| Would life have been more pleasant if you had not carried those grievances or resentments? | |

| Question | Answer |
|---|---|
| How have you contributed to or made a difference to the lives of others?<br><br>Have you lived your best life? | |

After you have reflected and written your answers down, you may start the second scenario.

## Scenario Two

Scenario Two begins in the same way. You are at the end of your life looking into the mirror, thinking back on your life. However, this time your mindset is different, and you know you have lived your best life. When you have that image clearly in your mind, please answer the following questions. Remember to be completely honest with yourself and include as much specific detail as you can:

| Questions | Answers |
|---|---|
| What does it mean to you to have lived your best life? | |
| Create an image in your mind of your best life. What does it look like? What does it feel like? | |
| What are some of the beautiful memories you created? | |
| How does it feel when your life flashes before you? | |

| Questions | Answers |
|---|---|
| How did you live? | |
| What did you do? | |
| What were the things that you were afraid of but did anyway? | |
| What are you most proud of? | |
| What made the biggest difference in your life? | |

| Questions | Answers |
| --- | --- |
| How did you contribute to the lives of others?<br><br>Write an in depth description about your best life. | |

You should now have a description of your best life. Next, ask yourself the following questions related to the seven key areas of life. By focusing on these key areas, you will be able to create balance and harmony in your best life.

| My Health | <ul><li>How would my body feel if I was in perfect health?</li><li>What do I need to change to have perfect health?</li><li>What do I need to do immediately to change my health?</li><li>What do I need to do to create a better mindset – how can I have better mental and emotional health?</li></ul> |
| --- | --- |

| My Work | <ul><li>If I could do anything, what would I do?</li><li>In what way/s could I contribute to the world or serve others through my work?</li><li>What impact would I like to leave on others through my work?</li><li>How would I feel when I am doing this work?</li><li>What could I start doing immediately to bring me closer to the work I would like to do?</li></ul> |
|---|---|
| My Wealth | <ul><li>How much money would I like to earn? (A good way to do this is to write a list of all your needs and your wants and then add up how much that would be).</li><li>How much money would I like to save?</li><li>How much would I like to donate to others?</li><li>What could I do to bring me closer to earning this amount?</li></ul> |
| My Spirituality | <ul><li>What could I do daily that will connect me to my Spirituality?</li><li>What do I need to do to raise my level of awareness, my consciousness and my potential?</li><li>What will I begin to do immediately?</li></ul> |

| | |
|---|---|
| **My Relation-ships** | • This section may be broken up into different areas - intimate, family, friends, work, social.<br><br>• Who is important to me?<br><br>• What are the characteristics that are important to me in terms of the relationships in the different areas?<br><br>• What type of people do I want to surround myself with?<br><br>• What will I bring to people in my life – what type of friend, partner, family member, and colleague would I like to become.<br><br>• Write a description of how you would like your relationships to be. |
| **My Home** | • What does my home look like?<br><br>• How do I feel living in my home?<br><br>• What type of environment have I created in my home?<br><br>• Who would I like to be living with in my home?<br><br>• Why is my home my sanctuary? What do I love about my home? |

| My Social Life | • Who/ what type of people are in my social circles?<br><br>• What do I enjoy doing socially? What would I like to be doing as entertainment?<br><br>• What does "fun" mean to me? Who is in my "fun" circle?<br><br>• How much time do I spend socializing? |
|---|---|
| Interests & Adventures | • What are my interests?<br><br>• What adventures would I like to go on?<br><br>• What could I do to start doing something that I am interested in now? |

Nothing will change unless you take charge and become the change. You need to implement the necessary changes within yourself and your life to live the life that you truly want to live. The bottom line is that you are responsible for your life, for the decisions that you make, and for the way you use your mind to improve your life. Nobody else can make decisions for you, and nobody else can create for you. It's up to you. If you've been blaming others or circumstances for your life, it is time to stop. You are the only one responsible for your life.

There might be areas that you would like to change, but they won't change immediately. That's okay. When you write them down, you are imprinting them in your mind, and you are telling your subconscious mind that you would like to change that area. If you do this exercise, you will notice that you will start to get ideas about steps that you can take to make that change.

Once you have written your answers down, reread what you have written and connect emotionally to your responses— really feel what your life would be like if you made these changes. What is it like to live your dream? Consider the actions that you have identified in each of those questions— what you could do today— and begin at once.

Next, write a list of what you could do this week, and make sure you do it. At the beginning of each week, re-examine your answers. Ask yourself:

- Is there anything that I need to add to my answers?

- What can I do today to ensure that I'm living my best life?

- What can I do this week that will bring me closer to my dream life?

If we do not take actions every day toward our goals, we waste opportunities to create and live our best life. And what is the rest of your life? It is an accumulation of days. Therefore, what you do today is extremely important to your life.

Keep the first script. Often with exercises like these, it is advised that you get rid of the negative, or the one that you don't want, and I do agree with this idea. However, for this exercise, I would like you to keep the first script. I would also like you to revisit that script occasionally, for two reasons: First, so you can assess what things you may be doing in your life that you missed the first time you did the exercise or that need to be improved. Second, as an important reminder, to keep you on track. It is a self-assessment on whether you are moving forward toward your exceptional life or if you have slipped back into your old lifestyle habits. If you do find yourself slipping back, that's OK, as long as you reassess and get back on track.

When you get off track, please remind yourself of the importance of living your best life by re-reading these words from Steve Jobs:

*"Remembering that I will be dead soon is the most important tool I've encountered to help me make the big choices in life.*

*Almost everything - all external expectations, all pride, all fear of embarrassment or failure - these things just fall away in the face of death, leaving only what is truly important.*

*Remembering that you are going to die is the best way I know to avoid the trap of thinking you have something to lose. You are already naked. There is no reason not to follow your heart.*

*No one wants to die. Even people who want to go to heaven don't want to die to get there. And yet, death is the destination we all share. No one has ever escaped it, and that is how it should be, because death is very likely the single best invention of life. It's life's change agent. It clears out the old to make way for the new."*

- Steve Jobs

21

# I Must Have Been out of My Mind

*"When something is important enough, you do it even if the odds are not in your favor." - Elon Musk*

In this chapter, and throughout this book, I will share with you some of my experiences. You may or may not relate to them, but take whatever you need from them so that you may reflect on your own life, where it is currently, the emotions that you are having, and what you would like it to be.

What can happen in only eight short months is mind-boggling. Eight months prior to writing this book, I left a secure job in senior management. To many people, the role appeared to be the dream. I was working for a fabulous organization with a brilliant manager who was also a great person. I had a great CEO, wonderful colleagues, and a nice six figure salary to take home. I was happy, comfortable, and hadn't had any financial concerns for several years.

Despite this, I couldn't shake the nagging itch of discontent. I yearned for more, and as time went by, this gnawing became stronger.

I am an extremely sensitive person. I feel all emotions to their extremes, sometimes to the point of destruction. The thing with sensitive people is that we also have very strong intuition, if we allow it to come through and trust it to guide our actions. Intuition is also referred to as 'that gut feeling' you get about something. Gut feelings (or instincts) are a pain in that if you don't listen to what they're trying to tell you, inadvertently you find yourself heading down the wrong path. Trust me, I know, and as a result, I have learned to quieten the logic of my mind and listen to my gut, even when it seems to be saying something illogical, risky, or just not very sensible. I must have been out of my mind to leave such a great job, right? Let's be clear— I am NOT advising you to do the same! Not yet, anyway. We each have to follow our own path. In this situation, my gut continued convincing me to take a leap of faith and trust in the Source that lives deep within all of us — call it God, the Universe, Spirit, or whatever you are comfortable with; to me they are one and the same.

Driving in the morning traffic, spending most of the day on automatic pilot and then coming home to cook, clean, and go to bed, only to wake up and do it all over again the next day was draining the life out of me. Although I was going to a great job and performing to a high standard, I knew I wasn't doing my best. I was no longer passionate about what I was doing, and this was the sign that I needed to stop— for my life's sake. However, the conundrum was that my sense of loyalty to the company was at odds with my true desires, so I felt guilty about leaving yet knew I'd suffer if I stayed.

The joy of living, in many ways, had gone. I was no longer waking up with energy and gusto. I remember how passionate I used to be about that work, thinking about it all the way to the office with ideas popping into my mind and the excitement of working with my team to implement those ideas. Without that, there was no point in continuing.

24

To quote Steve Jobs again:

*"Your work is going to fill a large part of your life, and the only way to be truly great is to do what you believe is great work. And the only way to do great work is to love what you do. If you haven't found it yet, keep looking. Don't settle."*

Although I was probably meant to feel satisfied, the feeling of being trapped grew as the days went by. I felt like a prisoner living in a so-called land of freedom. The best parts of my days were taken, and I had been left with a small amount of time for my life, for the people I loved, and for the activities I enjoyed.

I had wanted to quit years earlier but various monetary responsibilities and constraints kept me stuck. I didn't want to lose or go backward financially. I wanted to keep moving forward, yet that gut of mine kept telling me to stop. While my mind was telling me I was crazy to even think about leaving my job and the money it brought, my intuition was screaming that I had no other option. For many years, I tried to mediate the David and Goliath like battle within me as my heart wrestled fervently with my mind. It was a big and seemingly crazy risk to take, yet I took it. David won the battle, so to speak.

I didn't know exactly what I wanted to do— at least I thought I didn't — but when I dug deeper, I discovered I did know. I had always known what I wanted to do, even as a young child. I wanted to work with people to help them find their passion and inspire them to make it happen. My natural gift had always been my ability to connect with others on a deep, spiritual level and being 'Miss Self Sabotage' myself, I had an instinctive knack for honing in on whatever a person's personal barriers were. Throughout my life, I would often reach certain levels of success only to find myself ending relationships, fearing people, and feeling unworthy— to the point

25

that I would ruin the success that I had managed to achieve. I had the talent, the ability, and the intelligence to achieve anything, but my subconscious patterns and fears would either only allow me to reach a certain level before crumbling, or simply not allow me to go further.

Being of service to people, inspiring them to believe in themselves and to take steps toward creating the life they want, had been my dream for most of my life. I also wanted to become a published author. This was an integral part of who I was. Even as a child, one of my favorite things to do was to write books and illustrate them. I had so many books that I had written and illustrated, and I loved them all. I wish that I had kept some of those books, just to be able to go back and remind myself of what I was born to do. After all, don't we all need that reminder, from time to time?

I did make a few attempts at writing in my adult life but never completed any until this very one. As well as becoming a published author, I yearned to work for myself. I didn't like answering to anyone, asking for permission to take a day off or take a vacation. It is my life. Shouldn't I be able to live it as I choose?

We grow up with messages from our family, our teachers, media, and society about the way things should be, what we should do with our lives, how we should behave, what we should look like, and what our level of self-worth should be. We become conditioned to think and live in a certain way so much that we don't even realize that these were someone else's messages. We just accept them as fact, and they become ingrained on a deeply subconscious level in our mind.

Sometimes, these messages are so embedded within us that we don't stop to question them or to think about what they mean for us, whether they are right or wrong, or where they came from. We rarely reflect on how these messages affect us and our life, and we rarely challenge them to think about the possibility of whether there may be another way, or whether there might be other thoughts that we could adopt. No matter where these messages came from, it is our responsibility to change them. It is our own responsibility to change our mindset so that we can change our life.

Bob Proctor often states, *"Two percent of people think, three percent of people think they think, and ninety-five percent of people would rather die than think."* What he means by that is that most of us live our lives unaware that we have been conditioned. We are psychologically habituated to keep doing that which we believe we 'should', in spite of the persistent negative outcomes, rather than asking the right questions that lead to a deeper level of thought and understanding of who we truly are and the potential that lies within us.

Most of us function through the kind of thought that gets us through the day — the kind that is in line with what we generally accept as our reality. This type of 'thinking' is rational and deliberative. This means we can consciously "observe" it and use it to analyze, make logical deductions and deliberate calculations. However, few of us engage in the kind of thinking that exists below our level of conscious awareness — real thinking.

Sometimes these thinking patterns are acquired at a young age throughout our schooling. Education is very important — I value and am deeply grateful for the education I received — but often education systems focus on classroom obedience and students are judged by their understanding of the work that has been presented to them, or the mark that they achieve on a particular test or paper. The education system is not designed to assist the child to understand their true potential. As a result, the child grows up thinking that their worth is a measure of the mark that they

27

received back at school. The thoughts they begin to believe about themselves in regards to that mark they received many years ago back in school then determines the results they will continue to get in life.

As a result of this type of conditioning, sometimes they may end up feeling like there is a box that they need to fit into, to be accepted. No child was born to fit into a specific box. Every child is special, unique, and gifted in their own way. And every child was born to contribute to the joy of this world by expressing that uniqueness.

There is a place in this world for everyone's gifts. In fact, the world needs that kind of diversity. No one person is better than another; we are all equally important. Can you imagine a world with an education system that recognizes and celebrates the unique talents and capabilities of each child, rather than just their ability to sit still, listen, and regurgitate lessons? The world misses out by not having a system that works for all children, not just the ones who are able to adhere to the status quo and excel in math, reading, and writing. These subjects are important, but only as important as the other skills, gifts, and talents which children inherently have.

It is often the children who are labeled as 'different' or who don't fit into the traditional education system who are brilliant. Nikola Tesla, one of the most powerful and brilliant minds in history, spoke of how, as a child, he would often have visions which he described as being real, even though he could not touch them. As an adult he used those visions as inspiration for his many sophisticated and ingenious experiments. [1]

Albert Einstein is known to have been unable to speak until he was four and read or write until he was seven. He was deemed dyslexic and autistic.

---

1 Taken from https://www.quartoknows.com/blog/quartoexplores/nikola-tesla-in-childhood

Another famous example is Isaac Newton who, although brilliant at Math, did poorly in almost all other subjects. The impact and difference that Helen Keller made on the world, even though she was deaf, blind and mute, is truly phenomenal. The beautiful and talented Katherine Hepburn was suspended from school on account of her non-conformist, rebellious nature. More recently, renowned airline tycoon, Richard Branson, who left school as a teenager, revealed that he too was dyslexic. Then there is Tesla Cars magnate, Elon Musk, who has been referred to as one of our finest and most important entrepreneurs alive today; he was diagnosed by doctors as hearing impaired because of his tendency to 'drift off' and disengage from those around him when he was a child. Musk was also bullied at school because he was 'different.'

These are all examples of people who didn't fit any conventional behavioral or educational mold during the school years yet turned out to be the greatest innovators, inventors and visionaries of our world. The world would not be the same place it is today without the brilliant minds and passionate hearts and talents of these people and countless other 'misfits' who have gone on to do remarkable things. It would be wonderful to see an education system that accepts and embraces difference in children so that more young people grew up proud of their qualities rather than ashamed of them. This would also make them more confident as adults focusing on their dream, and in turn, our world could benefit from their unique abilities.

The saddest thing is that the negative messages we receive in childhood are often carried into adulthood, preventing us from revealing our God-given gifts to the world. Instead, these messages become ingrained in our minds, and often, we live our life using up only a tiny fraction of the magnificent and infinite potential that lives within each of us.

# What is your mind telling you about your dream

*"The biggest adventure that you could ever take is to live the life of your dreams." - Oprah Winfrey*

By the time we become adults, we often stop listening to ourselves and our hearts. Sometimes, we are so consumed by responsibility and routine that we lose that natural inner joy; we dim the light that we were born with. Being an ambitious dreamer, I am excited about our potential and what we could do with it. I am excited to learn about people's passions and talents and the thing that lives inside them. One of my favorite questions to ask people is:

## What would you do if you could do anything?

Although there have been a few people who are genuinely happy and fulfilled with where they are going and are doing what they love for work and in life, the first thing most people say is, *"Well, I wouldn't be in this job, that's for sure!"* When I press further and ask them if they are able to leave their job, and what is it that they would do if they could, they tell me their dream. However, sadly, some don't know what that dream is. Most of the time, they express that they thought they knew what they were meant to do when they were young, but with all the conditioning,

31

messages, and paradigms that they have been living with for years, they have disconnected from their dream. They continue to work in their job and continue feeling miserable or unsatisfied. The fact is that most people believe there is no other way, but what they don't realize is that belief is a choice. And like all choices, a belief can be changed to be self-serving and positive.

Although my parents lived in poverty and lacked opportunity growing up, my father had big dreams for his children to succeed. Because I got good grades at school, he dreamed that one day I would become a doctor. He would always talk to me about that when he'd ask me what I wanted to be. Being the dutiful daughter, I would tell him what he wanted to hear. Actually, I never wanted to be a doctor; it didn't interest me at all. I wanted to work with people, but to teach, to write, and to be on stage. I always felt I was born to connect with people and help them see their beauty and potential. However, what my father did for me was extremely powerful. He taught me to dream. He taught me that anything was possible and that there was always opportunity for me to do better and to be better, even if at times it seemed impossible.

I would dream of becoming a teacher or a performer, a gymnast, of being on stage with people watching me, of doing humanitarian work on the other side of the world. As an adult, this deep passion for focusing on a big dream that people felt was impossible is still a big part of me. Being a dreamer meant that I had a deep desire to be better as a person, to learn, and to expect that which I aim for to materialize when it is the right time, particularly in my professional life. Being a dreamer has also helped me understand that no matter how bad things get, things can always get better if you use your mind — or imagination. It is often the imagination that takes you to the next step to make the impossible possible. I have had many experiences in my life when a big dream and vivid imagination have helped me manifest things that seemed impossible.

One of the most profound experiences occurred when I was twenty-two years old. My desire was so great that logic had no choice but to step out of the way. I had just completed my Bachelor's in Psychology, and I wanted to travel the world. At the time, it seemed impossible, but for many years I'd yearned to go to Europe to live and work in the UK. It was an epic dream for me because I had only ever been to Serbia twice as a child with my parents and grandmother. I had never even lived on my own before, so going to and living in a foreign country alone would be a challenge. Throughout my life, I had always had my parents there to support me. To some, this may seem insignificant or small, but for me it was a big deal.

Besides that, I was broke. I had given up my part-time job to focus on my final year of university studies and nobody that I knew of (at least in my small community) had embarked on any kind of adventure halfway around the world, much less done it alone. I was expected to complete my studies, get married, and start a family. That was what all the 'good' Serbian girls did, after all. But I wasn't ready for marriage; I had a dream that I simply had to realize.

Surprisingly, my parents didn't argue with me about living overseas, but that was probably because they never believed I would actually do it. The notion was just too big, and I'm quite sure they thought I was in la la land- off with another fantasy again.

Nevertheless, I did my calculations and worked out that I had six months to save $10,000, which was the amount I needed to get me overseas. That meant that I needed to find a job that paid $500 per week. Minus living expenses, I would have enough to make it happen. I didn't care what I had to do to get that $500 per week, I would scrub toilets if I had to, I just knew I had to get it. Despite $500 a week in Australia at that time being a considerable salary, and unlikely to be the kind of money you would get from cleaning, my dream, and perhaps the naivety of youth, defied logic. I was convinced I would get that money. I remember standing in the kitchen talking to my mother about how much I would need to go abroad, and that I was thinking about getting a cleaning job. She laughed out loud — nobody made that kind of money fresh out of college, much less a cleaner. Was I nuts?

I spent the rest of the day working on my resume and thought about where I could go to ask for work. There was an industrial area a couple of miles from where we lived, and they had recently built distribution warehouses there for the local shopping malls. I decided that I would submit my resume to every one of those warehouses. I parked outside the first one and nervously walked toward the front door. I desperately needed a job, but I was very shy and insecure, especially when I had to speak with someone older or in a position of authority. I saw two men in suits smoking in front of the building outside the front door. One of them noticed me approaching and asked who I was. By then, my nerves had taken over me, so I can't recall much detail, but I did manage to say that I was looking for work and would be happy to do anything, including clean toilets. He took my resume and said he'd pass it on to the operations manager, so I thanked him and left.

When I got back to my car, I sat there for a few minutes shaking. I knew I had to repeat this process for all of the warehouses in that street, to increase my chances of landing a job. I walked to the next place but couldn't get in on account of the boom gates. I didn't dare approach security, so I headed back to the car and sat there trying to contain my nerves, but they wouldn't settle, so, disappointed in myself, I drove back home.

Approximately a week after I had submitted my resume to that man who'd been smoking in front of the warehouse, the phone rang. I picked it up and, to cut a long story short, it was one of the executives from the company telling me that a position for an accounts manager position had opened up and was I interested in applying.

*"What? An accounts manager? Is he talking to me about an office job? Even though I have no experience. Really? Wow!"* There I was banking on cleaning toilets, thinking nobody would ever hire me for an office job, yet here they were! We arranged a time to meet for what I assumed was to be an interview.

When I arrived at the distribution center, I was walking through the car park about to enter the yard, and I noticed a boom gate. As I tried to walk through, a security guard stopped me asking who I was and what I was doing there. When I explained that I was meeting with the Operations Manager, he asked me to sign in. He called the manager on the phone, and only then did he allow me to walk through to the office. Funnily enough, I hadn't noticed the boom gate when I was there submitting my resume weeks before.

I met with the Operations Manager and although it felt more like a discussion than an interview, I was so anxious and shy the whole time that I was convinced I'd screwed it up. As I was walking out of the office, I bumped into the same man I'd given my resume to. I discovered that he was in fact the CEO. By chance, luck, or my own will manifesting this, the day that I submitted my resume, I had somehow, unwittingly, bypassed the guard and gone straight to the CEO of the company. I was mind-blown. I mean, what were the chances? So, I ended up getting the job... and it paid $530 a week!

It wasn't until after I had started working there that I discovered through reading the company policy that the security guard was never supposed to have left that security booth. He should have been stationed there the whole time, but for some reason, he hadn't been there on that fateful day. The serendipitous chain of events that ultimately led me to getting the job that would fund my trip abroad was a classic example of Paulo Coelho's famous words: *"The Universe conspires to help the dreamer."*

Of course, I had a marvelous time traveling, living, and working in the UK. I have stories and wonderful memories that I will cherish for the rest of my life. But apart from the fantastic experiences that I had on that adventure, I gained so much more intrinsically. *I learned that with a decision, determination, belief, and action, the rational and logical moves out of the way while the Universe steps in to help you get to where you are heading.* I now know this deeply, and I came back with the firm belief that I could achieve anything, if I truly wanted it. That was the biggest lesson I learned, and it has guided me thereafter. I had experienced magic for the first time, and I knew that I could experience it over and over again. I came home a different person; I developed a profound understanding of who I was at my core and of life in a way that I couldn't articulate at that point in time. But most importantly, I expanded my belief in the unknown, and in Source, in a way that was unbreakable. From that experience, I inspired others to step out and do what they really wanted. I now know that a deep dream, a determined mind, and the courage to act allows the Universe to respond and prepare the way for you.

I could never understand people who just accepted their miserable reality, convincing themselves that that's all there is, and things just cannot and will not get better. *"That's life,"* you would hear them say.

My intention is not to undermine or ignore the situation of people who are going through terrible experiences. We are alive as human beings to experience the full pallet of colors that is life, and being alive means allowing yourself to feel all emotions. Contrast is a Universal law. We all have our dark nights of the soul, and this is a natural part of life. Without experiencing the dark, we might not appreciate the light. Difficult times often force us to assess our situation, and often, through adversity the birth of a new idea, a new way of being, a new mission or purpose, is born. These times allow us to reflect, to assess, and then conceive a new reality for ourselves and maybe even for others.

During these times, we need to allow ourselves to feel the emotions, and to tread lightly and gently. Being gentle with ourselves during these times is critical, but we must also be diligent about the thoughts we are entertaining. We must ensure that they are not the self-deprecating, hateful thoughts that convince us we aren't good enough. Those thoughts are unnecessary, untrue, and do absolutely nothing to serve us in our attempts to become the best version of ourselves.

### *What about Your dream?*

In my line of work I meet many people who know what they want and would love to step out and do something different; they have visions of dream jobs, relationships, or life in general. Sometimes though, when you ask people why they aren't doing what they would like to do, the answer reveals that their deep subconscious paradigms are in control. When you dig deeper, you realize that all their excuses are associated with fear — the fear of not being good enough, fear of losing, fear of being hurt, and fear of being rejected. In today's world, this fear is amplified by the constant messages portrayed in the media and society. Most of us are brutally critical of ourselves but would be appalled if our partner, boss, or anybody talked to us in the same way.

Please know that I am not advising you or anyone to simply quit work and go for your dreams. For me, quitting my job was the only option at the time because that inner knowing inside me continued to get louder. I knew that it wasn't a rational decision, but I also knew that whatever happened, I would be all right. I have developed that inner knowing and self-trust over many years. You have your own intuition and inner guidance, and you know what is right for you. What I am saying and what I would like to gently and lovingly nudge you toward is making the decision about what you truly want— what would make you truly happy— and then step out and start working on that thing.

You could start working on your dream while you hold on to your job; you could start by simply putting aside an hour a day to work on your goal. Explore that new career path, do that course, develop that website. If it is love or a dream relationship you yearn for, start understanding yourself first and why you are attracting the people or relationships you are now. Start to change what you need to within yourself, and then step out and go on that date. If it is writing that book, get up an hour earlier, or take that week's long vacation as I did, and just start writing. These small steps are ways that you can work toward your dream gently, if you are not quite ready to quit your job just yet. Putting the small steps in place might make it easier for you to start taking some bigger steps toward your dream and living your best life. Remember to pay attention to the thoughts that dominate your mind and what type of messages they are feeding you. Are they giving you a false and destructive message, or are your thoughts positive and supportive of you? Notice your thoughts and bend them to your will — let them empower rather than discourage you.

We all admire those who take life by its horns and say, *"Fuck it! You only live once. Let's just do it!!"* They conjure a sense of awe in us, and we want so much to be like them — courageous and determined. They are the risk takers, the doers, the rain makers, the people who feel the fear but do it anyway. These people remind us not to settle for comfort because the real magic happens outside of your comfort zone. They are a great reminder that training your mind to focus on where you want to go will bring you so much more than allowing it to focus on the aspects of your life that you dislike.

These people make the impossible possible. They are the 'mumpreneurs', the mountain climbers, the inventors, the record breakers, the ones who have overcome countless setbacks. They are the people who are naturally shy and insecure but end up being fabulous public speakers. They are the parents who are pushing their own boundaries to become better, to live better. They are the doctors, teachers, and Wall Street executives who decide that they want something more, so they embark on an adventure to travel or start a charity. They are the factory workers who decide they deserve something bigger, so they go out and get that degree or open up that animal shelter. They are the ones who fail many times yet get back up again, ready to give it another go, ready to put their boxing gloves on and go for another round. These people have the eye of the tiger, a stronger will and a deeper desire. They are focused, and their higher faculties overpower any fears.

This inspiring person is in all of us. It just takes courage and the willingness to take the first step and not let your thoughts get in the way when the going gets tough. Remember, you are never a failure if you step out of your comfort zone to manifest a dream and you keep trying. History is full of champions who failed many times and through persevering achieved great things. Edmund Hillary was a great example of this. He

39

failed twice before he made it to the summit of Mount Everest. We all have a Hillary inside us when we develop our will, imagination, desire, and belief to be strong enough, and when we use our mind to work for us and not against us.

If you feel that you have a deep desire or dream for something different or more, I cannot stress enough how important it is to get a mentor or coach and an accountability partner. A coach will believe in you and keep your vision, particularly when your paradigms start to kick in and you feel like you want to quit. Every successful person I know has had a mentor or a coach. When I was working in management, I always had a supervisor whose function was very similar to that of a coach. I was accountable to this person, and they held a vision of where I needed to go even during challenging periods when I could not see what the next step was.

Your dream is extremely important to you and your life. I know beyond a shadow of a doubt that you can achieve that one thing that you would like to do or become. It doesn't matter what your history is or what story you have made up about yourself, you can do it but it is so easy to quit. It is so easy to allow our subconscious paradigms to continue to control us even though they are self-sabotaging. If you quit and give up on your dream, you risk living a life of 'what if's' and 'if only's' instead of looking back at your life with a sense of pride, accomplishment, or, at the very least, the courage to have given it your best shot.

We humans are interesting creatures. As brilliant, amazing, wonderful, ingenious, and remarkable as each of us is, we are often a juxtaposition — we carry the opposite and can be mean, self-sabotaging, fearful, and even violent toward ourselves and others. But this is a choice; you can follow your brilliance, your intuition, your positive self-talk, or you can follow the destructive and negative patterns.

Sometimes it can be a challenge to flip over to the side of your mind that sees your brilliance, beauty, and greatness in a given moment. We have all experienced unhappy events in life; however, allowing our past experiences to dominate our current life does not serve us in any way.

If I could say only one thing that I know for sure, it would be that each of us was born pure, beautiful, and perfect. Unfortunately, due to our external influences and our deep paradigms, we forget this somewhere along the way. That is the saddest thing because, even as adults, each of us still has incredible beauty, light, and genius within us. These innate qualities may be hidden due to our mindset, but they can never be abolished. The problem is our minds are so full of harsh self-criticism, fear, and conditioning that we often cannot see past this.

We all have a guidance system within us, the voice of Source - our intuition that never leaves us - if we are willing to allow it to speak and ourselves to be still and quiet for long enough to hear it. And once we hear that voice, if we are brave enough to step out and follow the direction in which we are guided, even if we feel fear, we begin to experience things that we may have never imagined. We all have a deeply connected, deeply knowing voice; it is the voice of Spirit, of Source, of God. We must choose to listen to it.

How do we connect and hear this voice within us? Different people do this in different ways. Personally, I learned to strengthen my inner voice by putting my focus and attention on it. I have learned to trust it, and the more I trust it by taking actions according to its direction, the stronger it becomes and the better it serves me.

Sometimes, if I am not clear about the message or the direction, I invite my inner voice to speak to me. I often notice it through a feeling in my stomach — that good old "gut feeling". I ask it questions, and I listen for the answer. At times, when I have felt worried, I opened up to it and felt its guidance and protection. I had to practice tapping into my intuition, particularly when going through difficult times because that is when the mind is clouded, and less receptive to positive influence. During these times, it is extremely important to be still and quiet and, for me, it is a time to commit more firmly to my daily practice of prayer and meditation.

## What Would You Do If It Was Guaranteed That You Couldn't Fail?

This exercise has been designed to encourage you to start dreaming and begin connecting to your intuition. It is a way to allow your ideas, creativity, and heart to flow without the criticism and fear of your mind. If your mind tries to take over during this exercise with its chatter and negativity, which it will probably try to do, let it go without getting caught up in it, and without letting it take over. It is normal to have some of this chatter as that is the function of the brain. Just don't buy into it. In such situations, acknowledge the unwanted thought, thank it, and then imagine wrapping it up with love. What works for me while I do this, and I would invite you to try this too, is listening to music that I love and that speaks to my heart. Meditative or relaxing music without too many lyrics is most helpful. I also like to light a candle; it creates ambience and elicits a relaxed feel.

Make sure you are in a place where you will not be interrupted.

Take a few moments to relax your body.

Starting from your toes, feel and relax your muscles, working your way through your body to your head.

42

Relax all the beautiful organs within your body.

Now, relax your mind. Tell it there is nothing to worry about. There is nothing that needs to be done right now. You are completely safe. This is your time to feel comfortable and relaxed.

Connect with your heart. Tell it how much you appreciate everything it does for you. Thank it for pumping blood throughout your body and keeping you alive.

Your heart allows you to experience beautiful emotions and the beauty of another person, of music, art, and other areas and situations that make a difference in your life. Thank your heart for the love and enrichment it helps you experience.

Lovingly invite your heart to talk to you.

Tell it that you are ready to hear its messages and its guidance.

When you feel that you are connected with your heart, ask it the following questions:

- *If I could do anything without fail, what would I do? What is that thing that would make my heart sing?*

- *What is the thing that I was born to do?*

- *How can I serve you, my heart?*

Have your Your2Minds journal near you while you are doing this exercise. Write down whatever comes to you from your heart in response to these questions. Be mindful of your thoughts during this process. What is your mind saying to you? Are there any interrupting or dominant thoughts? Write them down in your journal too.

Once you have completed this exercise, read the thoughts you've written down. Ask yourself:

- *How do I change them?*

- *What is stopping me from taking that first step?*

- *What could I do today to take that first step?* Write it down and set some time aside to do it. The first step does not have to be a big one; a small, easier step is better than not taking any action at all.

Practicing awareness of your thoughts and writing them down is important because it allows you to connect, identify, and recognize what you need to do. By identifying them, you can work on changing them.

Practice this exercise as often as you can. Sometimes, the answers may not be clear the first few times you do this exercise. This may be because you are not used to the process. You may not be accustomed to connecting to your heart. You may even have been living your life through the fear driven chatter of your mind. That is okay if you have. Practice this exercise, and practice listening to your heart's message to yourself. The more you practice, the stronger your messages will become. By a message, I mean a thought or, predominantly, a feeling. Your feelings will tell you if it is the right thing for you. You may feel excited by the message, and you might even feel the excitement mixed with some fear. This shows that you are on track because the message you're receiving to do the thing that excites you is probably a big thing that you may not have ever achieved, or even attempted, before. It is natural to feel fear when we are embarking on new journeys.

# Your 2 Minds

*"The human mind is constantly attracting vibrations which harmonize with that which dominates the mind. Any thought, idea, plan, or purpose which one holds in one's mind attracts a host of its relatives, adds these 'relatives' to its own force and grows until it becomes the dominating motivating master of the individual in whose mind it has been housed." - Napoleon Hill*

April 2017, the decision was made, I was going to become a Proctor Gallaher Institute (PGI) Consultant. I hadn't been engaged in full time work for over three months. Although I had been enjoying the "me time" to wake up whenever I wanted, walk on the beach, and go to the local cafe and just read, I had never been without work, so the reality of not receiving a fortnightly pay check started to kick in. I knew I wanted to run my own business, one in which I could inspire and work with people so that they could realize their potential, and I knew I wanted to write. Becoming a PGI Consultant was exciting; it would train me to deliver Bob Proctor's twelve lesson program and assist people to refine their goals and finally transform their self-sabotaging paradigms, thereby allowing them to have the success in life that they had always dreamed of having. This had always been my passion and one of the reasons why I chose to study psychology at university. I was interested in people, in human behavior, and in helping people break through their own negative patterns.

Initially, I was very excited, but shortly after my enrolment in the PGI training course, my own deeply embedded paradigms began to rear their ugly heads. I became overwhelmed with anxiety, fear, and shame. My inner voice started to rant at me:

*"What if you fail at this, what will people think?"*

*"Suzana, you have tried to do things before, and they haven't worked!"*

*"Perhaps you should just return to full-time work again? But that would mean you are a failure. How embarrassing!"*

*"Everyone will be talking about you. Everyone will think you're a loser!"*

Imagine my powerful paradigms screaming at me, combined with the fact that I had no income, and you can imagine the state of panic that ensued. I continued digging my own self-deprecating psychological black hole; I would wake up around four o'clock every morning overwhelmed with anxiety. Some nights, I was literally praying to get through the night without dying. Panic attacks can do that to a person. The emotional and spiritual pain I felt started to manifest into physical pain. It was a living nightmare.

My vibration at this stage was so negative that it was affecting all aspects of my life, including my relationship. To add to the turmoil, I had suffered a miscarriage the previous year. I had always wanted to be a mother and had I not miscarried, the baby would have been born right about then, in the midst of that horribly anxious time. When the baby's due date came around, I had this overwhelming need to be alone and I felt I had not grieved properly after the miscarriage— I needed a day to myself. Things went from bad to worse when, while out for a walk, I bumped into a dear friend who had given birth to her baby son only three weeks earlier. What a stab to the heart that was — another one. Did God have it

46

in for me, I wondered? Had I done something wrong? Everything seemed to be going against me, and I couldn't understand why.

I went from having had it all to losing everything (at least that's how it felt at the time). The worst part was that I was losing hope, my dreams were fading, and so was my once unshakeable confidence. I was in a dark place, and I felt like I would never get out of it. As vulnerable as I feel sharing such personal and intimate details of my life, it is through our courage to tell the tale that we can connect and see our strength. I confess that there were some especially bleak days when I even thought about taking my own life. Fortunately, with the help of some wonderful people, I kept putting one foot in front of the other, one very small step at a time. Looking back, I see the reason for my descent into that deep, dark hole: inside, I felt completely unworthy. I was afraid, and I did not believe that I could be a success in business, or life. On some profound level, I was more concerned about what the world would think of me rather than what I wanted. Ultimately, I had allowed these hateful thoughts and feelings of unworthiness to take me captive and entrap me.

It was in the midst of this dark period that the concept of *Your2Minds* as my perfect business idea was born. I had been seeking a business name for several months, but all the names that came to mind, for one reason or another, did not feel right. Then one day, while lying on a massage table, I finally allowed a state of relaxation to enter my mind. It was during that massage that the name *Your2Minds* came to me like a bolt of lightning. I remember walking out feeling, for the first time in all those dreaded months, a sense of excitement and direction.

So, why Your2Minds? What is the significance? Well, there are several reasons, and they vary from literal to figurative. For me, the name Your-2Minds signifies:

47

- The 2Minds all human beings possess: the conscious and subconscious.

- The two voices in our head: one voice telling you that you are great, you can do this, and the other voice telling you that you are unworthy and incapable.

- Being in 2Minds: when you are unsure about something and you are finding it difficult to make a decision.

- The power of 2Minds working together to create something significantly bigger and better. Two people fully focused and in harmony pushing each other forward into greater and bigger realms, or two people fully focused and working in harmony to create a significant idea or project.

I had used all of these areas previously, and I knew that I could also use these to get myself out of the terrible rut that I was in. I knew that to change anything, I must have daily discipline. I did this by practicing the exercises that I had in my PGI 'Thinking Into Results' program. This extraordinary program works on changing the negative, non-serving beliefs that are deeply embedded in your mind. By permanently changing these beliefs, or paradigms, you will see a change in your attitude, behavior, and, ultimately, your results. Life just works when you know how to use your mind. You can create changes in any area of your life that you want to by learning how to reprogram your mind.

It was not until I had explored some of the concepts in *A Course in Miracles* that I recognized that I had completely lost trust — trust in myself, trust in life, and trust in God. I realized that nothing would change until I developed my faith again. I had to push that discipline in my daily study and practice further. I had to reconnect to my inner core- my Spirit- and I did this by:

- Continuing my Thinking Into Results lessons every day.

- Practicing *"Let Go and Let God!"* This was an affirmation I repeated over and over again, and as I did so, I would envision all my inner organs that were holding tightly on to fear letting go and relaxing.

- Doing daily mirror work, affirmations, and story scripts.

- Praying with a partner (it's amazing what one prayer with two people intent on resolving my issue did).

- Sharing this situation with my amazing meditation teacher. She would connect with me regularly and encourage me forward. She was an accountability partner of sorts.

- Getting daily support from my best friend, whom I trust and who has always been there for me through thick and thin.

This all might sound like a lot of work, but when you are in such a low state, you need to have the mindset that you will do whatever it takes to get out of it. It's like any principle of success; it takes a firm commitment, action, and a determined attitude, which means being prepared to do whatever it takes. Of course, as is usually the case, the work was worth it in the end. Shortly after combining all this, I noticed something had lifted, and a week or two later, I was approached to do some consulting work. I had funds to go to Toronto to do my training with Bob Proctor, and my relationship with my partner improved dramatically. It all happened at once, but it had taken me shifting my mindset and silencing my old non-serving paradigms before I could experience the change. I had to lift my vibration to what I *wanted* rather than what I didn't want. I had to become the person that I wanted to be in my mind first. I had to do this with trust and faith that everything was going to fall into place. And so it did. It is absolutely phenomenal that when you do the work to change your subconscious paradigms, by changing your mindset and lifting your vibration, the things you have wanted just flow to you easily and naturally.

## Your2Minds Exercise

*"If you want to find the secret of the universe, think in terms of energy, frequency and vibration." - Nikola Tesla*

This book will delve into each of the previously mentioned Your2Minds concepts and guide you through some powerful exercises to help move you forward in any area that you would like to apply them to. Each section has a broader dedication to these areas. For now, please think of an area in your life that you may find a little challenging or that you would like to work on to get exceptional results. Please work through and write your answers to the following questions in your Your2Minds journal.

- What is the area that you would like to focus on?

- What has happened previously when you have tried to get better results in this particular area? Explain.

- What results are you getting in that area? If there is a pattern in your results in this area, what do you think is the message or paradigm that your subconscious mind is holding on to? (It is usually the result that you get over and over again.)

- What vibration do you think you send out unconsciously?

- Are the thoughts you have about this area of your life positive or negative?

- How could you change these to messages that are more loving and would serve you better?

- Are you in 2Minds about this situation?

- Whom could you trust and work with as an accountability partner?

- Is there anyone that you would be able to work with on a spiritual level?

Answering these questions honestly is important. We can only change ourselves and our results by first understanding who we are and how we currently think. After you have answered the questions, and written down your honest answer to each, I would like you to write a detailed answer to the next set of questions. The more detail you go into, the more effective this exercise is because you are painting a picture in your mind of what you want it to be like. Having a clear and detailed mental vision and focusing on that image repeatedly with emotion and faith is one of the most powerful ways of manifesting. In this way you impress your subconscious mind with the image and the emotion connected with it. As a result, your behavior will change, your vibration will rise, and results WILL follow, provided that you are persistent.

To help you with this, I have included some exercises. Go through each of these questions by writing your answers down in your Your2Minds journal.

- If anything were possible, and you knew you would not fail, what results would you like to get?

- What pattern or habits do you need to develop to make this new way of being, or these exciting new results, a reality?

51

- What is the new positive message that you would like to develop in your mind, which will assist you in moving forward toward the results that you want?

- What are the feelings associated with these new results? How do you feel when you imagine yourself achieving these new results or this new way of being? Your emotions are very important because they will lift your vibration, and your vibration will propel you toward your new goal. The Universe will respond to your new vibration by moving the new result or new way of being closer to you when you start to step out into action. It is the way that the Law of Vibration, which is a primary Law, and the Law of Attraction, the secondary Law work.

- What will the new message from your mind be?

- If you are in 2Minds about a situation, make sure you take some time to clear that confusion up. Decide what it is you want and stick to it. You need to have a clear mind so that the Universe may respond, in turn. Otherwise, you will be sending out a vibration of confusion and a lack of clarity. Remember, the Universe loves order. If you have an accountability partner, get working with them, and check in with them on a daily basis ("The Power of 2Minds Working Together in a Spirit of Harmony" chapter includes a great method that you can implement with your accountability partner). If you cannot find an accountability partner at this stage, that is okay, too. Just keep doing the work. Become self-disciplined and do these exercises by yourself, for your own benefit.

# The Conscious and Subconscious Minds

*"Self-sabotage is like a game of mental tug-of-war. It is the conscious mind versus the subconscious mind where the subconscious mind always eventually wins."*
*- Bo Bennett, American Businesswoman*

Our conscious and subconscious minds have been studied by psychologists and philosophers for centuries, but it is Freud who popularized the subconscious mind in the modern world. He spoke about the different layers of the mind, where approximately ten percent of our thoughts are conscious thoughts, and the remainder reside in the subconscious and unconscious minds. Although we think that we are deep thinking beings, most of our thinking, emotions, behaviors, and results are below the levels of conscious thought.

Simply speaking, our minds function on two levels. One is the surface level, the level from which our thoughts stem; this is the conscious. The other, deeper level is the emotional level; it is our subconscious. Often, we are not aware of the subconscious mind, yet it controls as much as ninety-five to ninety-eight percent of all our behavior and the results that we consistently get in all areas of our life.

53

The subconscious mind, often referred to as the feeling mind, absorbs everything that we see, feel, and experience. It is nondiscriminatory and will absorb all the information and experiences around it. Luckily, our conscious mind, which is referred to as the thinking mind, can be used as a filter for what impresses your subconscious mind. By not allowing any emotion to be attached to the thing that we are experiencing, it is less likely to have an impact on our subconscious mind. The subconscious mind, once impressed, will control your behavior and your results. The good news is that the subconscious mind and its paradigms can be changed. One way is through repetition backed up by emotion, and the other way is through a strong emotional impact i.e. shock.

This is why when we have experienced a deeply traumatic event, our behavior often changes automatically. But just as negative experiences can change the subconscious mind, so too can positive, emotionally impactful events. This is both an unfortunate as well as fortunate matter. On the one hand, in life it is often a negative or traumatic experience that has the most impact. However, the fortunate part is that we can develop strong, positive emotion to influence and eventually diminish the negative impact that has been imprinted on the subconscious as a result of a situation.

We can witness the power of our subconscious mind in every area of our lives. When someone experiences a shocking or traumatic situation — being bullied at school, a car accident, or being bitten by a dog — it is likely that the particular reaction to the situation or circumstances associated with that event would become markedly different to what it had been prior to the event. For example, someone who experienced being bitten by a dog would likely develop a fear of dogs after the event, despite having had no fear of dogs prior. Similarly, a car accident survivor may develop a terrible fear and anxiety any time they got behind the wheel of a car, despite having been a confident driver prior. This is the subconscious reacting to that stimulus. That shock that is experienced during the incident, the intense feeling of fear and overwhelm was imprinted on the mind, and now, whenever they are put in a situation in which an object representing the cause of the shock or threat appears, the subconscious mind reacts, in order to defend against the stimulus and mitigate the threat.

The biggest change in my behavior that I can recall occurred when I was in London, after I had experienced a terrifying ordeal. I was working as a live-in carer for a marvelous and fascinating ninety-six-year-old woman, Agatha. Agatha had been the only child of an extremely wealthy Estonian family that had migrated to the UK when she was just a child. She inherited the entirety of her family's wealth and was fortunate enough to enjoy it. When she was younger, she had her own chauffeur and was whisked around in prestigious cars. Agatha must have been one of the most interesting people I had ever met. The stories she shared with me were so different from what I had experienced growing up in the working-class suburbs of Melbourne, Australia, and I thoroughly enjoyed them. Our worlds regarding upbringing, life experience, and social status had been miles apart, yet we managed to develop a special friendship within a short period of time.

Agatha lived in a four-story townhouse in South Kensington, London, full of immaculate interior decor and furnishings. I couldn't believe my eyes when she showed me her entertainment room; it was filled with exquisite, original artwork. Some appeared to be authentic Renaissance pieces. My favorites were four exquisite paintings of four beautiful Goddesses, each one representing a different season.

The evenings at Agatha's place were usually uneventful and quiet. We talked about the good old days, and as she shared intriguing stories of her life, she would read my cards. Agatha was quite psychic and did readings using a regular deck of playing cards. Some days, we would watch television and she'd be in bed by nine-thirty at the latest.

One day, I woke up with a terrible feeling in the pit of my stomach. Something was not right, and I suddenly wanted to leave that house. It seemed completely irrational to feel that way because I loved Agatha and enjoyed my time with her. I couldn't explain it, but I wanted to jump out of my skin. Something was about to happen, but I didn't know what. I got down on my knees and prayed with all the intensity that I could muster. I was desperate to leave but had no idea where I would go. The day went by and nothing happened, but that feeling of overwhelming discomfort stayed with me. The evening drew near, and Agatha and I sat in her lounge room enjoying the operatic genius of the Three Tenors on T.V. It was lovely, and Agatha stayed up past her bedtime. She was tapping her finger on her chair, and although she was clearly enjoying herself, I remember thinking how odd it was that she was staying up so late past her usual bedtime of nine o'clock in the evening. I never asked her, but I often wonder if Agatha also sensed something was off that day.

At exactly six minutes past ten, the doorbell rang. That too was strange because nobody ever visited at that hour. By this stage, my instincts were bellowing at me not to answer. As I walked toward the front door, the desperate voice within me urged me to retreat and ask who it was. I tried to use my rationale to convince myself it was ridiculous to ask who it was — it was probably just my boyfriend or one of Agatha's friends, I convinced myself. Why would I ask who it was? In reality, I don't know why asking who it was would have been embarrassing. In fact, I now feel stupid even having had that thought. I chose to listen to my 'logical' mind instead of my gut, and what a mistake it was.

To this day, over twenty years after the event, I can recall every thought that went through my mind. Deep inside me, I knew that what was about to take place was going to change my life forever, and I knew it was not going to be good. However, despite knowing that, I chose to listen to the rational part of my mind which was convincing me not to be ridiculous and just answer the damn door. That fateful decision saw me opening the door to three masked men looming frightfully over me in the doorway. The shock I felt was beyond comprehension. I screamed with terror. In that moment, petrified, I fully believed I was going to die. Funnily enough though, I was not afraid of dying. The fear I felt was for the thought that my parents would have to experience the loss of a child on the other side of the world. I knew I had to push past the masked men and somehow get out onto High Street, which was only a couple of houses down. High Street was always busy, and if I could only get there, we would be safe.

Unfortunately, even with all that adrenaline pumping through my body, I couldn't muster up enough strength to push my way past the three men onto the road. Instead, they pushed past me and entered the house. One told me not to fight them, and we would be safe. He took me to the room where Agatha sat and asked Agatha for her jewelry. Agatha remained impressively calm — after all it was just a man wearing a balaclava over his face standing in her lounge room — and told him that she didn't have any jewelry when she in fact had a lot of it and it was worth a fortune! One of her paintings alone would have set someone up for life. Despite the obvious untruth, to my astonishment the burglar didn't question it and left the room. I tried to hide the two silver rings that I had recently bought in Florence, Italy. They were not valuable, but they were precious to me, so I sat on my hands in the hope they wouldn't notice.

The whole ordeal was over quite quickly. When the man left the lounge room, Agatha grabbed the key and locked us both in the room. We got

57

on the phone and called the police. I was still completely petrified and couldn't even string a sentence together. The police arrived within minutes and did a search throughout the house. We were told that the men had run straight up to the top floor. There was a couple who lived above us, and as the burglars tried to break into their room, the man who lived there threw a kettle at them, sending the burglars fleeing. It turned out that Agatha's upstairs neighbor was actually a jewelry store owner, and he had planned to fly out to Dublin that evening to spend Christmas with his wife's family. Fortunately for us, that afternoon they had decided not to take that flight.

Ever since that incident, I've dreaded being alone in large houses. I despise the sound of doorbells, particularly at night. To this very day, when I do find myself in a large home alone, I have to be consciously aware of my thoughts and remind myself to stay calm, and that I'm safe.

Recently, I decided to stay at my parent's home while they were overseas on vacation. Their house is not large but still big enough to elicit this fear in me. My partner decided to surprise me by stopping by after work. It was late at night, and I was on the phone with a friend trying to work out my website. Although I heard the first knock, I ignored it. My mind and body immediately reacted in terror, and I began to shake. I was transported back to Agatha's house, convinced there were three masked men at the door waiting to barge in. I didn't want to face it, so I continued to ignore the knocking. I was petrified but knew I couldn't continue to ignore the now persistent knocking. If I didn't answer, maybe they would break in, and then I would have to relive the terrifying scenario I had survived many years ago. My imagination was running wild and, on some level, was preparing to relive the dreadful night in London. When I had regained some composure, I did the thing I hadn't done at Agatha's. This time, I asked who it was. I had learned my lesson and wasn't about to make the same mistake twice. *"Avon calling"* a familiar male voice replied. Relieved to hear the safe familiarity of my partner's voice, I opened the door and we shared a chuckle, but he immediately noticed how shaken up I really was.

This is an example of the power of the subconscious mind. The incident at Agatha's house in London had occurred some twenty-two years earlier, yet it still sends my brain and body into automatic flight response. The good news is that we can change the subconscious mind, and this is certainly one area that I must continually work on. I don't want to live the rest of my life petrified any time I am alone in a house and hear a knock at the door.

The other upside is that if the subconscious mind can be this strong and stubborn in the face of fear and negative events, it can also be used as a potent tool to create more positive outcomes for one's life. My personal example, albeit negative, clearly illustrates the power of the subconscious; one incident impressed my subconscious mind so deeply that even after more than twenty years, a stimulus triggered terror and sheer panic. The only way to stop this negative reaction is for my conscious input to change it. This means that if I impress my subconscious mind to work for me rather than against me, I will be able to positively impact the areas of my life that I choose to. Once I make that impression, my results will be permanent, unless I experience another event with a strong enough level of impact, or if I consciously work on changing that paradigm.

### How do you change your subconscious mind to benefit you?

As I mentioned earlier in the book, the two key factors that impact the subconscious mind are strong emotion and repetition. This is why mirror work, affirmations, dream boards, and writing your 'life script' (this is basically a written narrative of who you would like to become, or how

59

you would like your life to be) work so well. And when they are done with deep emotion and a sense of already being there or having that thing that you would like, they become all the more powerful. We do this by using our conscious mind to develop new, positive thoughts and emotions which render the old, destructive paradigms that no longer serve us redundant. If you don't know what your subconscious paradigm is, all you have to do is look at your behavior and your results. Your results will always reflect what is happening within you, at the deeper subconscious level. You will never change your results until you change your subconscious paradigms.

## *Changing Your Subconscious Mind to Benefit You*

*"Although we think that we are deep thinking beings, most of our thinking, emotions, behaviors, and results are below the levels of conscious thought."*
*- Suzana Mihajlovic*

This is a simple activity that you can use in any area of your life in which you want to get better outcomes than you have up until this point, despite your efforts. It is another reflective exercise for your Your2Minds journal.

1. Think of an aspect of your life where you have wanted to improve your results or change your behavior but have struggled to do so. Write it down.

2. Write down the results that you usually get in this area.

3. What is your mind telling you about this area? Write it down.

4. Write down how you would like to behave and what kind of results you wish to see.

You might have a longer version of this first, and if you have, that is great.

5. Now write down what you would like to change and turn it into a one sentence affirmation as if it so already, beginning with, "I am so happy and grateful now that..."

For example:

"I am so happy and grateful now that I feel calm and safe in big homes"

"I am so happy and grateful now that I am earning $300,000 from my business"

"I am so happy and grateful now that my relationships are smooth and amicable"

"I am so happy and grateful now that I am a successful businesswoman."

You get the drift. Now it's your turn.

Using the statement "I am" is extremely powerful. Our subconscious inherently believes a statement with the words "I am" in front of it and will automatically elicit feelings and actions to fulfil the words you are saying to yourself. I have heard Wayne Dyer state that the response, "I am that, I am" was the response that Moses received when he asked God to reveal himself as He spoke to him through the burning bush on top of Mount Sinai. So, please be mindful of your thoughts, and be aware, very aware, of negative self-talk. Remember, the subconscious **does not**

**discriminate**. Whether your 'I am' is followed by a positive or negative statement, that is what your subconscious will absorb. So, after the words, "I am" — cancel any negative thoughts, immediately.

6. Repeat your affirmation as many times throughout the day as you can. Say it in the morning and evening in front of the mirror, with emotion.

   It is the emotion, as well as the belief attached to the words, that will really impress you subconscious mind. Without attaching emotion and belief to your affirmation, you are simply, emptily repeating words that have no impact on your mind. It is emotion, not just words, that lift your vibration, and belief shows that you are ready to receive. The emotion is telling your subconscious to prepare the way for you because it will happen.

7. Say your affirmations daily for a minimum of ninety days or longer, if required.

8. Write out your affirmations every day. This will only increase their power.

Years of social, cultural and psychological conditioning have created your paradigms and controlled your results up until now, so changing them is not an overnight fix, nor is there a magic pill that will make it happen any quicker. Just like anything that is worthwhile and that renders real, long-term change, it will take time, effort, and consistency. Be patient. Be persistent. And trust the process. The change you will eventually see in yourself and your life is worth the effort and persistence. Your life is worth it. YOU are worth it.

# The 2 Voices in Your Mind

*"Your biggest challenge isn't someone else. It's the ache in your lungs and the burning in your legs, and the voice inside you that yells 'CAN'T,' but you don't listen. You just push harder. And then you hear the voice whisper 'CAN.' And you discover that the person you thought you were is no match for the one you really are." - Unknown.*

Unless you are the Dalai Llama and have reached a state of true spiritual enlightenment, it is likely that before making any new or uncomfortable decision you will have to wrestle with those pesky inner voices that provoke doubt, fear, self-loathing, and encourage you to stay in the safety and predictability of your comfort zone. If it ain't broke, why fix it, right? Change is uncomfortable. It is scary, unfamiliar and can be challenging. It doesn't matter what the decision is — whether it's related to your work, finances, relationships, buying a new home or going on vacation, those voices will start ringing loudly, like a poorly rehearsed chorus line of negativity and fear mongering. It will tell you that you cannot do it, that you've never done it before, that you're not good enough, not pretty enough, not intelligent enough, not loveable enough, not rich

63

enough. It will also try to impress upon you what you *should* be doing; you really should be saving for a rainy day, you should be more realistic, and that you're crazy for even thinking about doing that thing.

The first thing to remember is that this is all natural. It's what the mind does. Your mind's function is to produce thoughts and to alert you to what *could* happen, even though it may be wrong. Often the thoughts in our mind, particularly those that are negative and destructive, come from a place of fear, not a place of love. I have learned from my mentor, Bob Proctor, that most of these negative and deeply embedded paradigms have nothing to do with us and our potential. Rather, they have been passed down to us for generations. Our parents pass them on to us, their parents passed them onto them and so the cycle continues from one generation to the next. What that means, essentially, is that we tend to make decisions and live our lives based on the thoughts and paradigms of our ancestors. Thoughts and paradigms that, ultimately, have absolutely nothing to do with us!

Combine this with the expectations of society, our neighbors, the media, and again, the thoughts we are thinking are really not our own. They are not in our best interest, and they certainly do not reflect what we really want, what we are capable of achieving, and what we are worthy of having. Napoleon Hill said, *"A man whose mind is filled with fear not only destroys his chances of intelligent action, but he transmits these destructive vibrations to the minds of all who come into contact with him, and destroys, also, their chances."*

When I quit my job, my mind went into battle mode. One voice was saying, *"Way to go! You're so brave! How exciting. The opportunity to create a magnificent future awaits!"* while the other was shouting, *"What in the world are you doing? You really must be crazy! What if you fail?*

*Everyone will laugh at you!"* The problem was not that I was having these thoughts — after all, it was a huge and risky step to take — the problem was that I chose to listen to the latter, and that was the beginning of my downward spiral. This voice in my mind grew louder until it manifested into full blown, paralyzing anxiety. My passionate, joy filled, happy-go-lucky personality had been hijacked. The voice I allowed to dominate my mind had taken over my natural inner light. However, it had not been extinguished. Thank God, we can be safe in the knowledge that no matter what, the core of who we truly are can never truly be snuffed out. Mine had just been temporarily overshadowed and, in this case, dominated by inner fear and anxiety. In listening to it, I fed the fear rather than confronting and overpowering it with my own bright light.

The concept of our 2Minds talking and influencing us in two opposing directions can be found in many religious texts and teachings. Often these opposing minds are referred to as the angel and the devil talking to us. On one side, we have the angel trying to protect us, sowing seeds of love, compassion, and attempting to guide us in the right direction — the one that will allow us to see and experience our own inner light and the life that we deserve. On the other side, we have the devil. He is trying to deceive us by leading us down the path of inevitable self-destruction. He convinces we are unworthy and will never amount to anything. This type of thinking often leads to self-sabotage

In more recent philosophical theories, this dichotomy is spoken of in terms of the true self and the ego. The true self is that pure, trusting, and connected side of us; the side that comes from love. By contrast, the ego is the part of us that is ruled by our fears. The ego will hold onto its identity at any cost, and it will scream even louder when it feels you changing and letting go of your old ways. That is why real change requires discipline.

When the ego feels threatened, it becomes louder and fights, as does a deeply imbedded paradigm. The ego loves to tell you what you can't do, who you can't be, and it likes to falsely inflate itself in front of others. It likes to attack you, to attack others, and to focus on faults, whether real or imagined. It does this because it is afraid. It is afraid of becoming non-existent, of losing its identity, of what others think. It is fueled by fear.

When you are connected and aware of your true essence, or who you really are, you cannot help but feel love, peace, and appreciation. There-fore, as your awareness rises, you cannot help but radiate loving energy to all around you. You no longer respond from a position of fear because you understand that there is no reason to fear. It can no longer paralyze nor control you. You might have heard the saying that Love is the light, and where there is light, the darkness fades. By now I hope that I have convinced you of the fact that your core essence is built on unconditional love. This means that, at your very core, you are perfect. *You* are the light.

So, whether you call it Your2Minds, the angel and the devil, or the true self and the ego, they are all basically different versions of the same thing.

Although it is natural to have some fear, allowing fear to dominate our actions prevents us from living a free, exciting, and full life. Allowing fear to dominate us, as we have seen in the above explanation, will lead to self-sabotage and, in some cases, even self-destruction.

The only way to a free and joy filled life is through love and through the emotions associated with love: peace, serenity, appreciation, and so on. To truly radiate love, you first and foremost must love yourself. What does it mean to truly love yourself? It means that you pay attention to the thoughts you have and ensure that you are planting seeds of love, self-respect, en-couragement, and self-forgiveness, without guilt. It means learning about yourself and stretching yourself to fulfilling more of your potential. It means

66

allowing yourself to step out into fear to live your desires because you know that you are resourceful and have yourself to fall back on when the going gets tough. It means accepting and loving your beautiful body exactly as it is right now, respecting your remarkable mind, and taking care of your own needs— filling your own cup first. It means being in awe of your inner and outer beauty and your unique talents. Interestingly, when you start to love yourself unconditionally, life starts to love you back, and it will love you and serve you in ways that will leave you in amazement.

As I sat there in Peggy McColl's beautiful cottage admiring Mississippi Lake, I asked Peggy what it means to really love yourself, and a new conversation began. We talked about how truly loving yourself is similar to the unconditional love one feels for a child. This means recognizing their beauty, innocence, unique talents and abilities, and nurturing them through any setbacks they may encounter. You guide and protect the children that you love. You do not scold them when they are afraid but soothe and protect them. This kind of love allows the child's naturally bright light to shine upon their world, lighting up hearts through the love, joy, and spontaneity they bring. *This* is genuine and unconditional love. And loving yourself in this way is the path to true self-love.

My grandmother, *Baba Nada,* loved me unconditionally, and I always knew it. Whenever she saw me her face lit up and she would run to me with her arms wide open, ready to engulf me in their warmth. She also showed me how much she loved me through the gentle tone of her voice, her encouraging, positive words and loving actions. Actually, as a child I felt she was the only person that truly loved me unconditionally. She was the only person I felt completely safe to be myself with because in her eyes, I was perfect and could do no wrong. I don't remember a time when she scolded us. She loved us so much that the only words she ever spoke were ones of kindness; she was always telling us how wonderful, smart, and important we were. And indeed we felt important when we were around her. Because of the love that I received from this one person, I grew up with that love in my heart, and I attribute much of the confidence that I have as an adult to it. Her love for me taught me how to love myself and others.

The next time you notice your own two inner voices locking horns, which one will you choose to focus on? Ask yourself if what you choose to focus on is serving you. Ask it if it is loving to you. If not, change it. If the ego keeps fighting, as it so often does when it feels threatened, using self-trust, ask yourself honestly what you need to do to be more loving, or to listen to your kind inner voice, as opposed to the one that does not serve you.

## The 2 Voices in Your Mind Reflection

This short exercise is designed to make you think about how and when your inner voice talks to you, so that you may remember to acknowledge the fearful thoughts and change them into loving thoughts. Many of us have not thought deeply about what it means to truly love ourselves, and we may never have reflected on how we could love ourselves more completely. This exercise will help you look at the way you have been toward yourself and then change any destructive or unhelpful patterns to more self-loving and supportive responses.

Think about the following areas, and in your Your2Minds journal, note down the answers to the questions after you have reflected on them.

- What are some of the thoughts you are having that do not serve you and stem from fear rather than love?

- As you go about your day, notice your thoughts. Keep your journal with you and write down when you notice yourself having a fearful thought or a loving thought. At the end of the day, have a look at how many of each type of thought you had throughout the day. Are you surprised by any of these thoughts? Is there a pattern in the way you tend to think? How many have you written down? These thoughts have had a major impact on your life, and it is time to start changing them. How could you change your fearful, self-destructive thoughts? One way to do this is by thinking of a positive affirmation that would serve you. Write the affirmation down as in the previous exercise.

- Take a few moments to think about what it means to really love yourself. Write this description down in detail.

- Think about how you generally treat yourself. Are you loving towards yourself? Are your actions in line with what it means to really love yourself? If not, how could you change your thoughts and behaviors to be more loving?

- Imagine a child, another person, or animal that you love deeply and unconditionally. Would you talk to them the way you talk to yourself? Would you treat your loved one the way you treat yourself? If your answer is no, how could you change your self-talk to be more loving and more supportive? What could you do to treat yourself better— to honor, respect, and value that marvelous and important person that you are?

- Commit to doing one thing every day to show that you are being loving to yourself. What is something you could do?

When I notice myself succumbing to negative inner talk, I simply stop. I literally stop whatever I'm doing and refocus. If I'm at home, I light a candle, put my favorite soothing meditation music on and focus on the music for a few minutes. I then focus on my breath, my heart, and stomach. I move on to opening my heart and solar plexus areas. I open up to Source and allow myself to feel fabulous, powerful, unconditional love flowing to and through me. I keep my focus on my heart and Source and let this feeling flow. This is where perfection lives; this is our core. The truth is we are all intellectual, physical, and spiritual beings. No exceptions. Unfortunately, we are taught to focus on our intellect, and as a result, we tend to neglect our spiritual selves. Now is the time to start becoming aware of who you are— the real you — the spiritual one that has all the answers. It is time to connect with the perfection that lives deep inside you. It's time to allow your spirit to shine bright and bold. During this exercise, I remain focused on my spirit for as long as I need to, until I'm ready to stop. Every time I do this exercise, I get up feeling calmer, more relaxed, connected, and ready to go about my day with unshakeable confidence.

I encourage you to introduce a similar exercise in your life. If you are new to meditation, start by doing this for a few minutes only and gradually build up as needed. When you connect to your true self, to Source, you will feel grounded, peaceful, and inspired because you will have connected to the real you. Everything else is a virus— a lie! That negative self-talk has been lying to you all these years. Through this exercise, you will be guided and come to understand what your next step will be as you gain clarity and self-acceptance

Remember to write down any new insight, inspiration, or message that comes to you during your little meditation. You will soon understand the beautiful, bright genius that lies quietly within.

# Being in 2Minds

*"Indecision is the seedling of fear." - Napoleon Hill*

We all know that feeling when we are stuck between two options, and we find it difficult making a decision. Being in 2Minds about a situation is something most of us have experienced. It can be stressful, make us lose sleep, and impact all areas of our life if we allow the confusion to overcome us. The constant second guessing and doubt can be utterly exhausting.

If you are anything like me, when I find myself unable to make a decision, I ask someone I trust for advice. When I am uncertain about what to do in a particular situation, it is usually during a time when I am feeling insecure, fearful, or lacking in confidence. Being in an extremely confused state, and the emotion associated with indecision can feel like a real nightmare. In fact, the state of being this way is often so much worse and drains so much more energy than trusting yourself to make the right decision and trusting that you are resourceful enough to deal with the consequences of that decision.

In such times, it is especially important to be aware of your state of mind and to avoid second guessing yourself. Second guessing is debilitating and prevents you from making a 'true decision' - one that you make and firmly stick to. Indecisiveness prolongs the feelings of anxiety and confusion and does nothing to help you or the situation.

We all make decisions from time to time that, in hindsight, may not have been the best but, in every scenario, there is something to learn and evolve from, if we're open enough to the lesson. Often, other more powerful opportunities present themselves from a decision that we may have initially thought was a mistake. Continuing the self-torture of being in 2Minds blocks you from growth, self-love, self-respect, and your true infinite potential.

Living in a confused state of mind is not desirable. Clarity of mind and confidence create a more fulfilling life and allow for better decision-making. They encourage self-trust as you draw comfort from knowing that you will be okay and that you are not afraid to make mistakes. It allows you to recognize that you are a marvelous being with an equally marvelous mind. A clear state of mind allows you to develop your will and to focus on where you would like to go, rather than where you do not want to go.

A clear mind will show you the next step that you need to take. A frantic mind will only hold you in the same state of confusion, which may lead to further mistakes or stepping out into the dark, lost and without direction. By living with a clear state of mind and a clear vision of what you want, you are showing the Universe that you know what you want and are ready to receive. You are showing your worth, your courage, and you are allowing the Universe to respond to you, accordingly.

When we are in 2Minds, it is okay to ask for advice and honest feedback. There are many people who have walked the path before you and are already where you would like to be. I am sure there are people in your life whose wisdom, experience and results make it worth asking them, *"What would you do in this situation?"* These questions are important because they make way for a different perspective and the opportunity to learn from another person's experience. Moreover, through that conversation, an idea or solution may present itself that will help you make the right decision.

Ultimately, we are responsible for our own lives and decisions. So when you do ask for advice, be aware of why you are asking. Sometimes, we ask for advice because we feel that we can't make a decision ourselves. At other times, it may be an avoidance strategy — we *don't want to* make the decision and prefer another person make it for us. Many people simply haven't been taught from an early age how to make decisions for themselves and take responsibility for them. As a result, they often fear the consequences of their decisions and lack the self-confidence required to make a decision and stick to it once they have made it.

It is understandable that when we are in 2Minds, asking another person to decide for us may provide a solution; however, it is not *your* solution, and, therefore, you are giving away your personal responsibility. In a sense, you are giving away your power and the right to make your own choices for your life. It may also indicate that you don't trust yourself. You fear making the wrong decision, and the possible repercussions of that. In this case, you are failing to recognize your infinite potential and may feel you are ill-equipped to cope with the potential consequences of 'bad choices.'

If the above scenario sounds like you, please do not beat yourself up. Use this realization as an opportunity to learn more about yourself. Understand why you have developed this habit and where your fear of making decisions comes from. Ask yourself what you are getting from trusting others to decide for you over trusting yourself and knowing what is right for you and your life. While you do this, remember to be aware of the inner messages that are coming to you from your mind. Are they self-deprecating? Is your mind serving you, or is it sabotaging you? Don't let your mind go to the place that tells you that you're hopeless and can't do anything right. Just forgive yourself. Practice making your own decisions and owning them regardless of the outcome. It's ok to make a mistake. The more practice you have in making decisions, the better and quicker you will become at making them in the future. The more you practice, the less time you will spend in states of confusion and being in 2Minds. Always be mindful of your thoughts, and just keep practicing. Remember what it means to truly love yourself.

Being in 2Minds can sometimes mean that there are big decisions to make and the answer to these may not come immediately. They require contemplation and thought. This is different from being in a state of frantic confusion. In this case, the confusion, or contemplation, does not stem from insecurity, or a fear of making a decision alone, or even a lack of self-confidence. It comes from having to make big decisions, whether they be pleasant or unpleasant. It may be a decision concerning your health, your relationship, or a member of your family.

Sitting with the options and reflecting on them carefully may be exactly what is required. Periods that require big decision making can not only be very stressful but may occur during a time when there are other challenges that you are experiencing, such as grief over a loss, or a major change in your circumstances. These are times when we should indeed tread lightly and allow ourselves the time to feel the emotion and to process all the necessary information before making a potentially life changing decision. The important thing here is to ensure that fear and confusion don't overwhelm your contemplation and delay the decision further. It is also important to take steps to avoid overwhelming your mind and do something daily that will get you closer to the right decision. Once you have processed your options and made a decision, it's time to let it go and have faith.

## Making a Decision When You're in 2Minds

Being in 2Minds can be uncomfortable and downright annoying. So what do we do when we find ourselves in this bewildering state?

### Part A: Is being in 2Minds your normal state?

When you are in 2Minds about a situation or decision, the first step is to ask yourself the following questions — remember to use your Your-2Minds journal and to be completely honest with yourself, no matter how difficult or confronting that may be for you:

- Am I confused because I'm afraid of making this decision, and do I feel insecure about decision-making?

- Has the pattern of making decisions previously led me to further confusion or a state of being in 2Minds?

- Am I confused about making this decision because it will be easier for someone else to make it for me?

- Do I trust myself to make decisions?

- Do I believe that someone else would make a better decision for me and my life than what I would?

If you have answered yes to any or all of the above questions, I congratulate you for being honest with yourself; this is the first step to changing anything. The next step is to understand why you feel you cannot make the right decisions for yourself and your life. To know

75

yourself and why you do what you do allows you to move forward. As Lao Tzu stated, "*He who knows others is wise; he who knows himself is enlightened.*"

(If you answered No to all the above questions, congratulations, you can move to part B of this exercise below.)

Remember to write your answers down in Y2M journal:

- What is it that I am afraid of when making decisions?

- What is the cause of my insecurity and lack of confidence?

- Why is it easier for me to give this over to somebody else?

- What could I do to change this pattern? (It is important to actually try and be decisive when addressing this question. "I don't know" is not sufficient).

## *Part B: Steps to help you make a decision when you are in 2Minds*

Great! So, now you know why you find it difficult to make a decision. You are ready for the next step. This step is for everyone, whether your confusion stems from fear, or it is a decision that requires contemplation. Part B will guide you through a process that assists you in deciding any time you find yourself in 2Minds about anything in your life.

- Sit quietly. Completely relax your mind and body and connect to your inner core — this is where the answers come for me. You may want to do the little meditation from the previous chapter to help you connect within.

- Write a short description of your situation and what you are in 2Minds about.

- Write down a succinct question regarding the decision you would like to make.

  For example, "What do I do about scenario A (insert short description of scenario A here) and scenario B (insert short description of scenario B here)"? or "What is the right decision for me to make between option A (insert option A here) and option B (insert option B here)"? You may also have another preference you would like to use for your question.

- Close your eyes and sit quietly for a few minutes. Focus on your breath, and quiet your mind. Once you feel that your mind is quiet, and you are reasonably relaxed, ask yourself the question that you have written down. Allow answers to flow to you. Do not stop them but do not engage with them either. Just let whatever comes up flow through you. Using a different colored pen to the one with which you wrote your questions write down whatever comes to you at this time.

- Once you have written down all the answers, reread them aloud. Close your eyes again and relax your mind. Now ask yourself, what is the solution for me in this situation? And again, using a different colored pen, write out what comes to you. As above, try to remember that this is a free-flowing exercise, so do not let your mind get in the way. Just keep writing. Once you are done, reread all your answers out aloud again.

- Once you have completed the above exercise, put your journal away. You do not need to think about your problem or the decision you have to make until you go to bed. In fact, if you can, try to avoid thinking about it altogether. Put it aside and concentrate on becoming as relaxed as you can while you go about your day.

77

- Before you go to bed, go through the responses. You might even want to do the exercise again at this time. This would be recommended if you have the time because you may get a stronger sense of clarity by doing this another time. You might even want to put your list under your pillow. When we ask ourselves a question and do an exercise similar to this one before we go to bed, the question taps into our deep inner knowing as we allow our subconscious mind to do its work and to come up with answers for us. Often these might be the right answers for us.

- Once you have completed the exercise before bed, be sure you let the situation go. Don't think about it. Just focus on relaxing your mind and body and getting a good night's sleep.

- When you awake in the morning, before you get out of bed, write down the first thoughts that come to mind. Some of them may not seem directly related to the decision you are facing. Write them down anyway. Remember not to analyze or over think. When you have written down your thoughts, you may be pleasantly surprised to discover the answer to your dilemma. Often, after a good night's rest, with renewed clarity from having done this exercise the night before, an answer that feels right will appear.

- This exercise may be repeated over several consecutive nights, until you have a strong inner knowing that you have the answer. Sometimes, by looking back at the answers you had written down previously, you may come to realize that the answer was within them.

- Remember, the key to this exercise is to relax your mind and body and let the responses flow to you without allowing your analytical mind to overtake or sabotage this process.

# The Power of 2Minds Working Together in a Spirit of Harmony

*"Again I say to you, if two of you agree on earth about anything they ask, it will be done for them by my Father in heaven."*
- Matthew 18:19

It has been written that when 2Minds come together with one focus in a spirit of faith and harmony that which they are focusing on is guaranteed to manifest. I have experienced this repeatedly in my life. Something truly magical occurs when 2Minds come together. There is a certain power in the spirit of two who share the same focus in complete harmony. This power lies in the doubling of strength, of will and focus, and a magnified lifting of vibration. The vibration associated with the goal or end product takes a quantum leap in energy, and as a consequence, a quantum leap in results is produced. Our actions take on a stronger leap of faith and a quiet confidence because we are not only carrying our desire and dream but also the goodwill, faith, and focus of our partner. This is the strength and power of 2Minds with one focus working in the spirit of harmony, working to uplift and strengthen and carry the excitement of, not only their dream being realized but the dream of their partner. It is a magic that is propelled by genuine care and love, and through this spirit, we have a deeper connection to Source.

I have had many experiences when I have prayed with or shared my friend's vision and subsequently witnessed magnificent manifestations, as a result. One particularly memorable experience I had involved a complete stranger and I committing to a challenge to work together for ninety days, our ensuing friendship, and the miracles that came from that.

It was January 2016, and I was enrolled to do a course in Sydney when I received a call from a young man who was working for the company running the course. Our energy aligned on that call, and we began talking as though we had been friends for years. One of the things I noticed immediately about him was his desire to be of service, his professionalism, and his willingness to go above and beyond to help me out. During that phone call, we talked about our dreams, our goals, and the challenges that we experienced in reaching those goals. It was one of the most uplifting conversations I had ever had with someone, much less someone I barely knew. By the end of the call, we promised to help each other reach the goals we had discussed over the phone.

During that conversation, my new friend and I decided to conduct an experiment of sorts. We agreed that we would choose three goals that were big, that we had had difficulty achieving previously, and that required us to have a complete transformation in that area. The entire experience was mind-blowing. Not only did our friendship grow, but we truly realized the incredible impact of working in complete harmony with someone who is focused on assisting you to achieve your goal. The goals we spoke about that day were the big goals — the wild ones that seem impossible but linger inside us nonetheless.

My three goals were ones I had wanted to achieve for a long time but, for whatever reason, hadn't managed to accomplish. They were:

- To meet my soul mate and form a loving relationship

- To have a three percent consecutive return on my forex trading account

- To establish my own business and leave my job at the time

While they may not seem like a big deal to some people, for me they were epic. For one, my deeply imbedded paradigms about relationships meant I had a tendency to attract men who couldn't commit. On some level, those same paradigms kept me safe and offered me the perfect excuse to continue evading the need to confront my low sense of worth. But this avoidance came at a price; I had not been in a loving, committed relationship for over a decade.

The forex trading goal was big because I was a trading rookie and had never even managed a consecutive one percent return on my investment before. Every time I came close, I sabotaged my return by making classic rookie errors.

As for leaving work and going into business, well I'd never been in business before, I didn't have the funding I needed, I had no idea how to start, and, most importantly, I didn't know what on earth I had to offer. I knew deep down that I needed to leave my job and that I wanted to work for myself, yet I had no idea what my business would look like.

So, my new friend and I decided to help each other achieve our goals. When I mean help each other, I don't mean in the conventional way. We

81

had to take the required action to achieve our own goal, but we also developed a synergy that would propel both of us forward. It was that little ninety day experiment I mentioned earlier that we were excited about. Prior to starting, we set some compulsory tasks:

- For the period beginning February 1 to April 30, 2016, we would work in a spirit of complete harmony, complete faith in and support of our own and the other's goal.

- We would each carry with us a goal card with our own goal written on one side and the other person's goals on the other side of the card. My goals were written on the card as follows:

  *"It is April 30, 2016. I have exceeded three percent profits on my forex trading every month for three consecutive months."*

  *"It is April 30, 2016. I have set up my business name and my business."*

  *"It is April 30, 2016. I am dating my soul mate."*

  On the other side of my goal card, my friend's three goals were written out.

- Every morning when we got up, we would stand in front of the mirror and say our own goals aloud followed by our partner's goals. This had to be done with energy and emotion so that while we were reading the goals aloud, we could actually feel the energy and euphoria associated with achieving them. Additionally, we would visualise ourselves and the other person living their goal, and we had to lift our energy to that level of vibration for ourselves and them. It was like we were passing on the gift of this energy or vibration to the other person, knowing beyond any doubt that they were living their dream already.

We would meditate daily for a minimum of ten to fifteen minutes, first on our own goals and then the other person's goals. We would then send the other person uplifting energy, with a feeling of excitement about them having achieved their goal. We would see ourselves and them living with their goal achieved, just as we did with the affirmations in front of the mirror. We had to act as if it was already done, as if WE HAD ALREADY ACHIEVED THESE GOALS.

- Throughout the day, we would think about the other person and send them love and positive energy for the achievement of their goal. We would stop what we were doing at certain times of the day and send them and ourselves love and the vision of achieving the goal.

- Once a week, we'd connect over the phone. This conversation had to be positive, and we would check in to see how they were progressing and offer suggestions and ideas about what they might be able to do next. In situations where one of us was feeling flat, it was both our responsibility to lift the to a higher energy of the discussion to a higher vibration and finish off excited about our own and each other's lives, dreams, and who we were as people.

- If one person was feeling discouraged, needed some suggestions or advice, or needed to resolve something, they would call the other to talk it through and find a solution. It was crucial that we always left the conversation on a higher vibration than what we were on when we began.

83

There were times during the experiment when it felt too long, that the three months would never go by, and there were days when we felt discouraged, or the underlying fear of it not working would rear its ugly head. But we continued to get up each time we were down. We had made a commitment and promise to ourselves, as well as each other, and neither of us was going to quit until our 90-day 2Minds Challenge was over.

This experiment turned out to be a real turning point for me. It created miracles.

We started the 90-day 2Minds Challenge on the 1st of February. On February 14th, a mere 13 days upon embarking on the 90-day challenge, I met my soulmate. As I've mentioned, I didn't have a great history with relationships, so I didn't recognize immediately that he was my soul mate or whether it would even work out. However, this time I did not let that affect me in any way, I didn't question it nor worry about it. I just focused on where I wanted to go in life, without thinking about whether this relationship was the right one at the time. I refused to entertain the "what ifs'" in a negative way for one second. I decided to just enjoy this wonderful new person whom I had attracted. Somehow, the 90-day 2Mind challenge lifted my vibration to a more positive, natural, and free state, and I simply allowed things to flow. Having my friend's energy, support, focus, and total belief in me helped me lift my vibration even higher. The daily meditation also helped tremendously in assisting me to calm my mind and allowed me to enjoy the relationship and just 'go with the flow'.

Today, that same remarkable man I met remains a big and wonderful part of my life. If you had known me before I did the 90-day 2Minds Challenge, you would know that this is nothing short of a miracle. I had been to counseling, to psychics, tried a ton of affirmations, been on dating sites and gone on countless dates, but something was always lacking;

either I wasn't interested, or it didn't feel right, or the men that I thought I could perhaps be in a relationship with couldn't, or wouldn't, commit to me. This new, loving relationship was testament to the power of 2Minds working together. My challenge buddy and I had harnessed the combined power of our 2Minds and created a synergy and vibration that went above and beyond the limitations that I had held for years in my mind.

What about my forex trading goal? Well, I decided to learn how to trade because it was something that I knew nothing about, and frankly, it intimidated me. It was precisely because of this fear and intimidation that I knew it was time to get very uncomfortable and to challenge my mind in a way that I had never attempted to do before, thanks to my ignorance and self-misconceptions. I also wanted to learn how to give myself other options and have multiple sources of income, so that I never had to rely on the "job". However, shortly after learning a few of the strategies, I once again self-sabotaged. Just as I was nearing my target percentage of profit for the month, I would do something silly, like not analyze a trade before I put it in. Consequently, I would lose all the profit and, sometimes, even a little more. I had never reached anywhere near that three percent monthly return prior to the 90-day 2Minds Challenge.

Based on my pathetic previous experience with forex trading, the goal of achieving a consecutive monthly profit of three percent return should have been virtually impossible. Despite that, I always knew it wasn't — after all, other people were making and even exceeding that profit margin consecutively. I do remember thinking, *"How in the world am I going to do this?"* knowing full well I simply had to. At the very least, I needed to focus on it with all my energy because if I couldn't do it for myself, I could not very well expect my friend to do it for me. For the entire 90-day 2Minds Challenge period, I did a trade analysis every night, listened to webinars, followed the strategies that some experts used, and put in the trades I felt comfortable with. I was focused. I wasn't sure I could do it, but I promised my friend I would give it my all, and I did. I can't even remember what happened month to month, but I can tell you that I achieved a three percent return every single month for the three months that we were committed to the 90-day 2Minds Challenge.

So what about my third goal — the one that revolved around leaving work and starting my own business? Actually, it was the only goal I didn't achieve during the 90-day 2Minds Challenge. However, I was gob smacked when only a few short weeks after the challenge ended, my boss called me into her office to tell me that there was going to be a company restructure and my job would be affected. This was the break I was looking for, and since I couldn't make the decision to leave work myself, the Universe did it for me (I'm sure it was a way to test whether I was serious about my goal). I waited until six months after the restructure to take my package and leave the organization, but the decision had been made well before then. At the time, I didn't know what kind of business I wanted to get into. I knew I wanted the option of working my own hours from home, and if I could choose anything, it would be to work with people in order to help them achieve their potential. I just didn't know how to go about doing that.

I hope you can see by now how the power of 2Minds working in harmony for themselves and each other really works. The three goals that I set out for the 90-day 2Minds Challenge were far reaching ones for me. How I would achieve them was a mystery to begin with. To be honest, I doubted they would happen at all. In fact, I even questioned if the whole 90-day 2Minds Challenge would work. One thing I did know was that I would not let my new friend down. I was committed to doing it completely and fully, and if my dreams did not manifest from the exercise, I was certain that his would. I wanted wholeheartedly for him to achieve his goals. I could envision his success, and I could see him in a greater and brighter light than what he could see of himself. I believed unequivocally in his potential and was so excited about his upcoming success.

After the challenge, we stayed in touch and reflected with excitement on the work we had done together with the 90-day 2Minds Challenge. The experience did not only bring us the attainment of goals that had been seemingly unachievable previously, it brought us so much more. It brought us a great friendship, the excitement of working together on a project with another person, and it brought us pride for the fact that we had created something we had never heard of or done before — the 90-day 2Minds Challenge was our creation born of a random conversation we had as strangers over the phone back in 2016. It brought us belief in and excitement about the possibilities that can manifest when 2Minds unite in a spirit of respect, belief, and harmony. And finally, it brought us other ideas for what we could do for ourselves and other people.

I invite you to find a person with whom you could take on the 90-day 2Minds Challenge. If you do it completely with the right spirit as we did, I am sure you will see amazing results and learn some magical lessons along the way.

As I wrote this chapter, I went back to some of the messages my friend and I sent each other during this 90-day 2Minds Challenge. The most evident thing for me was the impact our daily communication had on each of us. Just reading some of the messages instantly put me in a higher and happier vibration. The value of this exercise is beyond words.

# The 90 day 2Minds Challenge

Now it's your turn. Who do you know that you would like to do the 90-day 2Minds Challenge with? Who do you admire? Who do you know that has an uplifting, positive energy? Even if it is someone you may not know that well, or someone you think may not want to work with you, I challenge you to approach them and ask if they would be willing to do the magical 90-day 2Minds Challenge with you.

When you have found the person with whom you would like to do the challenge with, give them this book and ensure that you both agree on being fully committed to your own and each other's goals. It is vital that you both follow the 90-day 2Minds Challenge rules. Again, you will need your Your2Minds journal to write out your goals and brainstorm new ideas and solutions. Use your journal to record any insights that come to you, any changes in emotion, frustrations, and any breakthroughs. By writing, you are allowing new insights and ideas to come to you, and at the end of your 90-day 2Minds Challenge, you will be able to read back through the notes you've recorded so that you may be reminded of how much you have grown throughout this process, and how you have benefited from the 90-day Your2Minds challenge. Following are the rules that you and your 90-day 2Minds Challenge partner will need to implement for the whole 90-day period:

89

- First, write a commitment letter that you each sign and keep a copy. There is a sample of this at the end of the chapter. You could use that or create your own version of the 90-day 2Minds Challenge commitment letter.

- For 90 days, you will work in a spirit of complete harmony, complete belief, and complete support of your own and the other person's goal.

- Write out your own three goals (or up to three maximum) on one side of a goal card. Write your goals out using the following structure:

  *It is (insert date). I am so happy and grateful now that I have... (insert goal)....*

  Then, on the other side of your goal card, write your friend's three goals..

- Every morning read your own goals and your partner's goals aloud with emotion in front of a mirror. Remember to do this with energy and enthusiasm. Feel and envision yourself and the other person achieving the goals on your cards. Visualize yourself and your partner living the goal and lift your energy to that level of vibration for the both of you. You are passing on the gift of this energy or vibration to the other person knowing beyond any doubt that they are living that dream.

- Meditate daily for a minimum of fifteen minutes. First, meditate on your own goals and then the other person's goals, and during your meditation, send the other person uplifting energy, feeling the excitement of them having achieved their goal. See yourself living you goal, too. It is done.

- Throughout the day, try to stop several times and send your challenge buddy love and positive energy for the attainment of their goal. Take some time to give yourself love, too.

- At least once per week, connect over the phone. This conversation must be conducted in a spirit of complete harmony, ensuring the conversation ends with a positive and uplifting energy. During this phone call you can monitor each other's progress and offer suggestions and ideas about what they might be able to do next.

- If one person is feeling discouraged, needs some suggestions or feedback, or needs to resolve something, commit to calling the other to talk it through and come up with a solution. Always ensure that you both take responsibility for ending the conversation on a higher vibration than what you were on when you began the conversation. If you are the person listening to the setback, remember to keep focused on what the solution may be for your 90-days 2Minds challenge partner; never focus on the problem. Approach the situation with understanding and compassion but always concentrate on the desired result and how wonderful it feels to have achieved it.

And if you do lose focus from time to time, think of what my dear friend said to me during our 90-day 2Minds Challenge:

*"….Remember, it's 90% psychology!!! Keep focused, buddy. You're on the right track."*

## The 90-day Your2Minds Challenge Commitment Letter

I….(insert your name here)….dedicate the next 90-days, beginning….(insert date here) and ending….(insert end date here)….to the 90-day 2Minds Challenge with my 90-day 2Minds partner….(insert partner's name here). For the next 90-days, I will work in a spirit of complete harmony and focus. I dedicate myself to the following actions for the entirety of the 90-day 2Minds Challenge:

- I will read my goals and my partner's goals aloud with emotion every morning and every night.

- I will meditate daily for a minimum of fifteen minutes on my goals and my partner's goals, as outlined in Your2Minds.

- Throughout the day, I will think about my 90-day Your2Minds challenge partner and send them love and positive energy for the achievement of their goal.

- At least once weekly, I will connect with my 90-day Your2Minds challenge partner over the phone. I will check in to see how my partner is progressing and offer suggestions and ideas about what they might be able to do next. I will take responsibility for my vibration and ensure I leave every conversation uplifted and positive.

I look forward to realizing my own goals and witnessing the realization of my partner's goals. I look forward to working in a complete spirit of harmony, and I take responsibility for my actions. I acknowledge that I am here to hold the vision and totally believe in my own goals as well as those of my partner. I look forward to the growth that we will both experience, as a result of this challenge.

Signed:

….(sign your name here)….

Date:

Once you have completed your 90-day Your2Minds Challenge Agreement, be sure to send a signed copy to your chosen challenge partner.

# A Quick Note on Repetition

*"You have jewels inside you that have been lying dormant for most of your life. The more deeply aware you become of who you truly are, the more you experience these jewels, which are far more beautiful and valuable than anything money can buy. Your inner jewels are indeed priceless. It is through the discovery of them that you will experience the real meaning and deep beauty of your life."*

*- Suzana Mihajlovic*

Now that you've completed your 90-day Your2Minds challenge, take stock of how you feel. I'm guessing you're on a bit of a high right now, feeling empowered, astonished by what you've achieved, and ready to go out and conquer the world. Congratulations! I'm so happy for you because that's exactly how you should be feeling.

However, many people complete the challenge and assume that the post completion effects of feeling so optimistic, powerful, and motivated will have a default flow on effect and simply seep into their lives without any further effort on their part. I'd be leading you astray if I said that the challenge on its own was enough. Don't get me wrong, this a very powerful exercise that can yield phenomenal results, BUT — and there's a big but here — the real power lies in the repetition of the principles and habits you've formed over the 90-day period.

"What? You mean I have to do this all over again?" I can hear you say. I know, it's an emotional commitment that takes time and energy. But it's so worth it, right? So the answer is a short but resounding — Yep! You need to do it again — and not just once, but every day for the rest of your life. Now I'm not suggesting repeating the actual challenge with a partner and going through the letter and the commitment vows and everything

93

else that that goes with it (though I do recommend doing the challenge at least twice a year), but it does mean committing to the new habits and mindset you've formed.

You see, everything I'm teaching you in this book is for life. There are no quick fixes here. Your *infinite* potential means that Spirit inside you yearns to grow, to become more, to flourish. True personal growth is a lifetime commitment. So you need to be ready to incorporate the principles into everything you do, and you need to commit to the daily work for the rest of your life. As soon as you stop doing the work, you stop growing and becoming more of who you were created to be. If you're not growing, you're going backwards. The beauty of committing to your own personal growth and having the discipline to do the daily work that is required, is that it's a guaranteed way of living a life that just gets better and better. You need to continue the daily discipline and commitment that you had throughout the 90-Day challenge — forever. That is how you will yield the results to create the kind of magic you're so capable of creating. That is how you will illuminate the world with the light inside you and keep it shining bright, always.

In my consulting sessions, this is the one thing I emphasize more than anything to my clients. Repeat, repeat, repeat. Repetition is actually the number one 'Secret' to making the Laws of the Universe work in your favor. The problem is that once the initial euphoria wears off, few people are able to maintain the motivation to repeat 'positive 'statements to themselves all day every day. The fact is you don't need to stand in front of a mirror saying affirmations for hours on end for it to work, but you do need to get into a subconscious habit of thinking a certain way, almost on autopilot. But the autopilot doesn't come immediately. It comes through your daily discipline and commitment to yourself.

94

I know the chapter 'The Conscious and Subconscious' delved into this concept but, just the same, let me explain a bit more. All you need to do to see proof of the power of repetition is switch on the TV, log into You Tube, Facebook, Twitter or Instagram. Repetition is used as a persuasive tool everywhere — the media, advertising, politics, you name it. Whenever people want someone to think the way they do, they use repetition as the persuasive strategy to make it happen. That's why politicians have catch phrases they repeat over and over when they are campaigning and want your vote; it's why ads for something you've googled once in your life suddenly pop up every time you log into your FB or Instagram accounts; It's why news reports formulate and reinforce the same opinions day in and day out. It's all done with the goal of manipulating you into believing something that you may or may not otherwise believe. Why? Because, it works. Boy, does it work!

Repetition reinforces a message until the subconscious accepts it as being the truth. Now I know I've been over this throughout the book a few times, but it's worth repeating for the very reasons I just explained — the more you read it, the more likely it is to sink in.

As basic as it may seem, simply repeating a message or thought increases its persuasive powers dramatically — whether the message is positive or negative (Just be aware of that — the Universe doesn't discriminate nor ask questions. Whatever your focus is, on a deep, subconscious level, is what you will get — whether it's good or bad). Unfortunately, it's the very simplicity of this action that often leads people to overlook it. After all, how can something so straightforward have such a huge impact? It's almost a case of 'too simple to be true.' Yet, countless studies have shown that the more often a statement is repeated, the more its validity increases — even when the person making the statement is flat out lying. This is another example of how incredibly powerful our minds are and how

95

much potential we have to become that which we want to be in this life. And this is exactly why persisting with the daily repetition of affirmations and positive thoughts is so crucial — especially when you don't believe them.

Ever wondered why you just can't stop thinking certain negative thoughts, yet it's so hard to believe the positive ones? A big part of the problem is that we are generally more inclined to believe the bad than the good, whether it's about ourselves or others. That is precisely why I've been so repetitive in drilling the importance of always being aware of your thoughts and the way you speak to yourself. Our thoughts and self-talk have power unbeknownst to us. What you think and say on repeat to yourself, whether it be good or bad, is ultimately what you will become. No exceptions.

The formula goes something like this:

Repetition > Truth > Validity > Persuasion.

This tells us is that the more we repeat something, the truer it becomes. The truer it becomes, the more validity it has. And the more valid we think something is, the more we are persuaded by it. This is something often referred to as 'the Illusion of Truth. 'Ultimately, it leads to the message becoming easier to understand and therefore more likely to be adopted as truth. When an idea becomes familiar to us, it then surpasses the conscious filters and allows uncensored penetration to the subconscious. The trick is to keep the message simple. The simpler it is, the better!

By using repetition you can shift the paradigms that hold you back and silence those negative, critical voices that tell you that you're not good enough, pretty enough, smart enough, fit enough, motivated enough — or whatever unhelpful and unloving 'not enough' thoughts occupy your mind. Repeating the thing you want to be in a state of the wish fulfilled (in other words a way that assumes you already ARE this thing) helps you bypass those stubborn conscious filters and persuade yourself wholeheartedly that you in fact ARE whatever it is you WANT to believe.

So you may not believe you are the absolutely, delightfully, wonderfully creative and unique being I'm saying you are right now, but if you repeat those words often enough, you will eventually come to believe them as deeply and wholly as I do. And they are true. Why would you waste your life and deprive the world of your gifts by hiding them?

To end this short but important chapter, I want to remind you that you are beautiful, and magical, and powerful, and creative, and 100% capable of all you want to become and accomplish — I believe that unreservedly — and whether you're an affirmations in front of the mirror person, a journaler, a meditator, or all of those thing, remember: repeat, repeat, repeat — until you believe it as faithfully as I do.

Through repetition, you shift your paradigms and create new, better and more powerful ones. Life becomes more fulfilling and joyful, and you begin to understand more profoundly who your truly are. Consequently, as you become increasingly aware of who you truly are — without the viruses and self-deprecating paradigms — the more you will experience the inner jewels that have been lying dormant inside you. These jewels are more beautiful and infinitely more valuable than any jewel money can buy. Like you, they are priceless.

# My2Minds — Experiencing Depression and Anxiety

*"Character cannot be developed in ease and quiet. Only through experience of trial and suffering can the soul be strengthened, ambition inspired, and success achieved."* - Helen Keller

Now, you may be thinking I sound self-indulgent, and I don't know anything about you or your life and circumstances. You may be fed up with people trying to tell you that things could be different. You might be even be thinking, *"Sure, it sounds nice that I am such an important part of the Universe, but that doesn't give me the answer to how I can pay my bills at the end of the month, or how I can get that dream job, or buy a nicer house for my family."* No matter what your situation is right now, I would like to invite you to keep focusing and saying to yourself:

*'....(your name)....did you know if you weren't here, the Universe would literally be out of alignment?"*

I am hoping by you doing this, by making this statement a daily affirmation and reminder to yourself, it will eventually resonate, and from that, answers might start to come through to your mind about your next steps.

99

There is a solution to all our problems, and unless we choose to start thinking right, unless we choose to start allowing ourselves to connect to our inner light, or Source, we risk becoming stuck. Once we allow our mind to open up to the possibility that we might be such an intricate, limitless, and important part of the Universe, we start to unravel our inner genius and our creative solutions.

So in case you are one of those people who may be thinking that it's all easy for me to say, I would like to share with you one of the challenges that I allowed to dim my light throughout parts of my life. I have already shared some of this in previous chapters, but I feel that it's important to revisit this here.

Depression and anxiety have been an on again off again battle for me throughout my life. For a deeply emotional person, depression can be a challenge. But I now recognize that I have a choice. I have a choice as to how I use my mind. I learned this through my mentor, Bob Proctor, and the Thinking Into Results program.

If you are currently experiencing depression or anxiety and feel you may be experiencing clinical depression, it is important that you seek the support of a health professional. Working with a good health professional combined with the Thinking Into Results program can do wonders, if you commit to it daily.

Being part of a migrant family from the working class suburbs of Melbourne came with many challenges. Looking back at my childhood, I believe my depression kicked in at a very young age. My parents were struggling with the battles that come with being newcomers in a foreign country with little family or support, a language they didn't speak, and forced to work extremely hard as factory process workers. Their focus was merely on survival.

As an adult, I now view my parents as heroes and, as such, have a new-found understanding and appreciation of their efforts and sacrifices. I cannot imagine the courage they must have needed to make the decision to pack up their humble belongings and leave their village in order to travel to the other side of the world, not knowing when or if they would see their families again, or anything about their new destination. There was no internet in those days and no opportunity to continue their education. Being forced to leave school at the age of fourteen so that they could help their families survive in harsh post war Serbia did not leave them much opportunity to learn anything about the world.

My mother told me that the first time she ever traveled to the capital city of her country was when she met my father. Being the eldest of four, her duty was to help her parents provide so that the family could survive. She wanted an education and had been a diligent student yet was pulled out of school because domestic duties called, as they often did for young women in those days. Education and travel were never an option, yet ironically, when she got married, she found herself boarding a plane with her husband and two-year-old child to a foreign land she knew nothing about. The only thing I could compare that with today would be to packing a few essentials and going to Mars without any knowledge as to where you were going to live, how to speak the local language, nor how you would survive once you arrived. My admiration for my mother and her courage is beyond words, as is my respect for my parents' determination to survive and have a comfortable life once they arrived in Australia. Giving their families a better life than they had, often through hard manual labor, was what my parents and many of the European migrants in Australia at the time did. Their determination and hard work allowed us, their offspring, the opportunity of an education and a life of countless opportunity.

In addition to the difficulties that the average migrant family underwent, we children were prone to harsh and difficult situations, particularly bullying. Even these days, when I think back to how terrifying it was for me to walk to or be at school, I'm saddened. I was afraid to leave the house but had to develop the courage to do so. I was bullied many times on my way to school or even just leaving the house.

One day, I was visiting a friend and was accosted by another neighbor, who was a year or two older than me. After we exchanged a few words, she attacked me. I was a thin child with a head full of thick, long hair which my attacker grabbed and pulled as hard as she could. By then end of the ordeal, she had chunks of my hair in her hand.

Another time, my mother asked me to go down to the store where I was chased by a couple of girls from the street; one was the younger sister of the girl who had pulled my hair out. They chased me on their bikes and attacked me. I fell to the ground, and the rubble on the road pierced through the skin of my knees. The cuts were deep, as evidenced by the amount of blood pouring out from my knees and down my legs. I picked myself up crying, too afraid to turn back, though just as afraid and humiliated to keep walking to my destination. I walked all the way to the store to buy that milk, in pain, with my knees bleeding profusely and people staring at me pitifully. These and other experiences associated with being the child of new migrants led to deep sadness, loneliness, and significant anxiety which followed me throughout my life.

As an adult, despite having both studied psychology and attending numerous therapy sessions as a patient, there were still times when depression and anxiety overcame me. Sometimes this would appear within social settings, sometimes it happened at work, and sometimes it would take over various parts of my life simultaneously. Even with all my qualifications and my ongoing commitment to personal growth, my paradigms were so deep that they simply became overwhelming. Eventually, I became completely consumed by a black hole that was very difficult to get out of and could swallow me up for many months at a time.

So, I am just like some of you are. I have one part of me that is very sensitive and was prone to depression and anxiety, and then there is the other side that is happy-go-lucky and can uplift everyone in the room. When you are stuck in such a deep and dark place, it is difficult to move out of it.

Being in such a wretched and helpless state can feel like a foreign entity has taken over your body. It is through sheer determination every single day — in some cases, every moment of the day — that I managed to dig myself out of those holes. It took effort, will, and dogged persistence.

Once you are out of that cloud, you look back on the experience and thank yourself for pulling out of it because you begin to see the beauty of your life again. You start to appreciate it. I discovered, no matter how difficult it was for me, and no matter how much I did not want to accept it, that it truly is my choice as to which of My2Minds I would listen to today and every other day for the rest of my life. That was the gift of the Thinking Into Results program for me. It gave me an opportunity to realize who I was and the great potential within me. During those difficult periods, I didn't want to accept that it was my choice; it was hard to do anything, let alone try to change my mindset. Luckily, I eventually accepted that if I refused to take responsibility for my own life and mind, nothing would ever change.

The past has no control over me now. Many of us have challenging periods growing up, but I do not have to give those fearful and deeply negative thoughts any control over me today. I know that I cannot and will not waste my God-given potential. If I am such a compelling piece of that bigger Universal puzzle, and if I have that greatness and glorious light deep within, I cannot afford to go there again. I must use as much of this light and greatness as I possibly can — for myself, for you, and for the Universe. It is both my obligation and my right.

I have learned that it is only by being my authentic self am I able to allow others to be themselves, and it is only through letting my inner light shine bright that I can allow you to let your light shine bright. It is only through stepping out and working toward achieving my dreams that I can serve others. By lifting myself up, I can then lift you up.

Again, this is a choice, and it requires waking up every morning and reminding myself of the many blessings that I have in my life. Gratitude is the key. Just being alive is a blessing in itself. No matter what is going on around me, there is always something to be grateful for. This new realization about my life and who I am requires me to focus on connecting to my light and allowing it to consciously shine throughout the day. It is about feeding my loving and supportive mind over my destructive, fearful mind, every day. It requires letting go of my paradigms and feelings of unworthiness and replacing them with the truth.

The truth for every single one of us is that we are *infinitely* worthy, deserving, and magnificent. That means we are worthy, deserving and magnificent *beyond measure*.

Now, please put this book down, and read that last paragraph again. Please read it quietly, and then read it out aloud. Read it in front of the mirror. Read it with your name at the beginning of the sentence. Read it until it resonates deeply within your core. Go to your Your2Minds journal and write down what you experienced inside you — what feelings and thoughts you experienced as your read these statements aloud. Absorb how powerful and beautifully profound these words are. Remember, these words are about the most important person on the planet, YOU.

## The My2Minds Exercise

The exercise for this chapter is a short yet profound one. It focuses on realizing the truth of who you are when you discover the viruses that have been in your mind, possibly for many years.

Quiet your mind for a few minutes. Again, you may want to light a candle and play your favorite meditation music while you do this exercise. In your Your2Minds journal, write down the full statement below in a bright, vibrant color, so it stands out. You may want to highlight it or use markers to make it pop. Remember to insert your own name in the spaces. Sit quietly and connect with your heart again and add any other statement of truth that comes to your mind. You may come up with one or numerous statements. Whatever you come up with is the right thing for you. Now, with your arms wide open, say the entire statement aloud in front of the mirror. You can re-do this exercise by writing out this statement as often as you like but remember to keep repeating your statement of truth as many times as you can throughout the day. We want the message to penetrate deeply and find a new home in the subconscious, so that you can stop living the lie and start living your truth. This is who you are; everything else is an illusion. It is a lie. Let go of the burden of untruth you have been carrying around all these years and start to live the life you were born to live by remembering your truth every single day. Imagine the beauty that you will be bringing to your own life and to the world by living this truth.

*You see, the truth is that:*

*YOU....(insert your name here)....are worthy beyond measure; you are infinitely worthy.*

*YOU....(insert your name here)....are deserving without boundary; you are infinitely deserving.*

*YOU....(insert your name here)....are magnificent beyond measure; you are infinitely magnificent.*

# PART 2:

. . . . . . . . . . . . . . . . . . . . . . . .

## A Your2minds
## A Lived Experience

# Mentoring Your Mind

It is a well-known fact that rarely can a person achieve great success without the guidance of a mentor, teacher, or coach. Although there is mention of some great and well-known mentors throughout this book, sometimes a mentor or extraordinary leader comes from the most humble and discreet places. In this section, I will talk about one of my greatest leaders, without whom I would not be the person I am today. The guidance and wisdom that I received from this great human being will remain with me throughout my time on this planet. Her remarkable example has survived far beyond her years and will continue to do so for generations to come.

You will see that this remarkable woman used many of the concepts shared in this book without ever being taught to do so. Through her story, additional concepts are drawn into the picture, such as using your heart, gut, and mind as three parts of an intricate whole that provide each one of us with the innate tools that we require to achieve anything that we set our minds to, even when the odds are against us.

You have these intrinsic tools deep within yourself. They were provided to you at birth so that you could navigate the path of your extraordinary life, so that you would be guided and equipped with the infinite ability to create what it is that you truly desire. You may need to sharpen your

109

tools due to a lack of use but know that they are always there. They are your birthright.

Through this remarkable woman's lived experience, you will also see the importance of letting grievances go and living with a mindset of love. Letting go and forgiving means that you are no longer carrying the heavy weight of that which you've carried all those years, poisoning your mind, your body, and making it more difficult to allow the Universe to work through you and to bring you the things that you have hoped for. This doesn't mean that you must never express your emotions, such as anger or disappointment, but it does mean that once you have expressed what you need to, you let go of it completely.

The following story will show you how gratitude and appreciation for everything in your life, whether it appears to be big or small, is extremely powerful. It gives an example of how when you choose to focus on gratitude and appreciation rather than what you lack, you realize that you already have everything, and you will never be without, as long as you continue to express true and deep gratitude and appreciation.

You will learn that by being yourself and adopting the concepts in this book, you will naturally inspire others. You will achieve this by guiding your mind to connect with your heart, gut or intuition. By guiding your mind to focus on love over fear or grievance, you will teach it to feel a sense of gratitude. Through this, you will effortlessly guide others to be their wholly beautiful and magnificent selves.

In doing the work in Your2Minds, you too may want to consider reaching out to a mindset coach or mentor. I cannot express how powerful having a mentor coach you through Thinking Into Results program and make this a part of your daily study is for living your best life. It is difficult to change deeply embedded subconscious paradigms alone. Hence, it is important to work with someone who will guide you, who can see your potential and can understand your blocks but, most importantly, who will be able to lead you through those paradigms to transformation. I hope you enjoy the story of one of the most incredible leaders and women I have ever known. Most importantly, I hope that it inspires you to keep doing the work in this book and to change your mindset to one that benefits you rather than sabotages you and your infinite potential.

# Baba Nada's Marvelous Mind

*"The most beautiful things in the world cannot be seen or even touched — they must be felt with the heart." - Helen Keller*

This is the story of one of the most marvelous leaders, humanitarians, and women that I have ever known and was so fortunate to have had in my life. I would like to share this with you because although this woman was born in 1919, had very little education and, judging from her life experiences alone, was unlikely to have been thought of as someone capable of becoming the remarkable human being that she was. This woman had such a strong influence and impact on so many that, even today, fifteen years after her death, the thought of her brightens up the heart. She was so powerful because she chose to use her mind to allow her inner light to shine upon others from one corner of the globe to the other. She touched everyone she met and, to this day, although she has physically departed this world, her bright light continues to shine on in the hearts of all who were fortunate enough to know her.

My Baba Nada, or Grandma Nada, was an incredibly influential, awe inspiring person. This unassuming little pocket rocket was wise beyond her

113

years, and despite all the horrific challenges she faced during her eighty-four years of life, her light illuminated all around her.

Born in 1919 in Southern Serbia, Baba Nada lost her mother at the age of seven and was left the oldest female in a house that fed nine people in a tiny peasant village called Masurica. From the age of seven, she was forced to take on the role of a grown woman and housekeeper. Her daily duties included producing food for the household by working on the land — milking cows, sowing crops, and ploughing fields. She accepted that role without question and with a maturity well beyond her tender years.

Baba Nada had a scar on her head. You could only see it if you were playing with her hair, and I saw it many times because she loved it when I scratched her head. She would sit there on her chair by the window of my parents' home and bribe the children she was babysitting with twenty cents to play with her hair and scratch her head. Although she loved her hair being played with, it was also probably a way to distract us and get a few moments of much needed respite because she was often babysitting nine children at once. The children were from various migrant families whose parents worked at the local factories, and because nobody else from the community had the support of a grandparent, they all left their children with my Baba Nada.

Baba Nada told me the story behind that scar many times. She had been working the land, preparing the soil for the seedlings to be planted when she got into an argument with her bad-tempered younger sister, who attacked her with a hoe. Although Baba Nada shared the story with humor, I often pondered how terrifying it really must have been for her at the time. I used to envision her as a child pining for her mother, as any child would in the face of such a confrontation, yet not being able to reach for that comfort and safety.

Something otherworldly existed within my Baba Nada. It was an unspoken quality, rare, invisible to the eye, but felt by all who came across her. It was a strength of character that I have not seen or experienced in many people. She was unique, and she never swayed or shied away from her uniqueness. A tiny woman in stature with a giant power within. A character who saw the best in people and inspired the same, in return.

I don't know whether this was something that had been refined throughout her life as she was presented with challenge upon challenge, or whether it was something innate. I believe she was born with it. It was just so natural, unpretentious, impossible to fake, and it came from deep within because she connected with it, and she allowed it.

Growing up and living as a peasant farmer in Serbia may not have been easy, but during and after the two World Wars, poverty was ubiquitous. The stereotypical gender roles were also very prevalent. At the age of nineteen Baba Nada was married to a young man her uncle had chosen for her. In those days, marriages were very much a practical arrangement and, in this case, my great-Uncle believed that my grandfather's family had adequate land to ensure that his sister would be provided for with the basics in life, which in turn meant that he didn't have to worry about her. And so it was done.

I remember her describing her feelings when she first laid eyes on her future husband — a tall, handsome, and well-dressed man. Another boy in the village had taken an interest in her, but it wasn't to be. My grandparents didn't have a happy marriage. This often made me sad, and even when I think of them today, I really wish that they had found the love they both deserved. They were opposites in every way. Baba Nada was a big, strong, bright personality who absolutely loved people, no matter their age, religion, gender, or nationality. She loved everyone and everyone loved her. She was also physically affectionate. She loved to touch and warm you with hugs and kisses and would sit talking with you as she massaged your hands. She always gave you her full attention.

My grandfather was a good but somewhat lost soul. Unlike Baba Nada, he was a quiet, private introvert. He did not like people and perhaps even feared them. He didn't enjoy anyone apart from close family visiting him in his home. He valued his space and did not like to be touched. We all knew that my grandfather had experienced a lot in the war and in life, yet we knew very little about him. He rarely shared anything about himself or his experiences, which saddened us because we all yearned to know him.

My grandparents' marriage was volatile. Often my Baba's gestures would be met with angry words. She craved attention and loving affection. The sad thing was that they were both unhappy, but for their generation and culture, separation was not an option.

Baba Nada told me about a time during the war before my father was born and my uncle was only a baby when her marriage was so bad that she decided to take her child and run away. She didn't know how she would do it, but she had to return to her birth home as it was unbearable where she was. She took her baby and started away through the nearby wood. She thought by going through there, she would be able to get to the nearest town without being seen. It was unheard of for a wife to leave her husband, so had she been caught, she would have been scolded by her mother in-law and disgraced. After some distance she heard what sounded like groups of people running by. She hid behind a tree and saw foreign soldiers not too far away. She knew that if they saw her, she and her baby would be killed. So she sat silently, frozen, and realized she had no other option but to turn back as soon as she could safely do so.

Her misery did not only come from a loveless marriage but also from having an alcoholic child. I attribute my Uncle's alcohol abuse to his own internal battles and pain. When he was not drinking, he was the most generous, loving, kind, and intelligent person that you could ever meet. Unfortunately, he died in his early fifties, and this was yet another grief that my grandparents had to endure. The two of them discovered his dead body on the floor of his apartment.

Naturally, it took time after my Uncle's death for my grandmother to smile again, but despite a deep and long period of grieving, she managed to find her light again. She really was an extraordinary and endearing character.

It never ceased to amaze me how this elderly woman, who knew only a few words of English, managed to connect with people from all walks of life. After her son died, it became extremely difficult for them to continue living in their home because my uncle had lived in the same vicinity, and he would visit them daily when he was alive. It had simply become too painful for them to be there. Because they lived in public housing (which in Australia can take years to come by due to notoriously long waiting lists) it would likely be a very long time before they could move into another property.

This did not deter Baba Nada. She went to the public housing office and somehow managed to explain her situation; it may have been through an interpreter, but often she just somehow got her message through despite her very limited English — a brilliant and determined negotiator she was! She explained to me that she had been told that the wait to be moved into another house would take a minimum of seven years, and unfortunately, there was nothing they could do to fast track her application. It was no surprise to me that a little less than a year later, she announced that they had approved her application, on bereavement grounds, to move to another apartment in a different area. How she managed it is beyond me to this day. But that is who my Baba Nada was. She had a magical way with people.

I will never forget one day when I went to visit her, around a month before she died. In front of the apartment block carpark was a big patch of grass where residents would often sit and play with their children. I saw my Baba Nada on the grass talking with and hugging a woman whom I had never met. The lady had just been shopping and was giving Baba Nada a bunch of bananas. I hugged my Baba and introduced myself to the lady. When I told her my name and that I was Baba Nada's granddaughter, she said in her broken English, "Maybe your grandmother, but she is my mother!"

The lady was an Afghani refugee who had recently arrived in Australia with her two young sons. She had no family in Australia and was escaping war in her homeland. Apart from her two young children, my Baba Nada ended up being her only source of connection and family in this new and lonely home of hers. Neither woman could speak English well, yet they managed to connect on such a deep level that the woman felt comfort, trust, and genuine care, which was simply astonishing. I guess the heart speaks a Universal language, and I knew that Baba Nada always spoke and connected from the heart. People know when they are loved, when they can trust, and when they are genuinely accepted. They can feel it. We can connect with others even if we come from worlds apart because we all speak the Universal soul language of the heart. And Baba Nada was as fluent in this as anybody could be.

You may ask why I have felt the need to dedicate an entire chapter of a book entitled *Your2Minds* to my grandmother. Sure, she was remarkable, but what does this story have to do with the purpose of this book? This story shows the power of mindset and the difference that your daily choices can make to your own and other people's lives. With all the trauma and hardship my grandmother endured in her life, many of which I have not included in this book, she chose to be who she was. She could have easily become a sad and bitter person. She could have chosen to lock herself away at home and become a victim of her circumstances. She could have complained about not knowing the language, about the people being different, about how much she missed her home country. Having had such a difficult marriage, an alcoholic son who would often become abusive and abrasive, and eventually losing him, she could have easily become depressed. Frankly, who could have blamed her? This would all have been justified and reasonable given the circumstances.

She also suffered from hypertension, high blood pressure, and there were times when she complained about her pain and grief, but her light, her belief in people, in God, and in life never diminished. She allowed her pain and grief to be present and to be with her, but she did not allow it to take away her spirit and determination.

Baba Nada knew the secret to life. What's the secret, you ask? There were several key attributes that my Baba Nada unwittingly possessed but the biggest and most important was her sense of gratitude. She was always grateful and appreciative, eternally optimistic, she was authentic and unapologetically herself, she never caved in to fear and, even during her most difficult times, her faith and conviction were unshakeable. She was not a religious churchgoer, but she believed faithfully that God was looking after her. She would thank Him for bringing her to Australia, she would thank God for her wonderful lifestyle, she was grateful for her health, she felt wealthy, and she knew that she was protected and had all that she ever needed and more.

It's interesting; my grandmother lived on a pension, yet she always had money and was unfailingly generous. One day we were on a tram together, and there was a woman sitting beside us with her toddler in a pram. Baba Nada started to play with the baby and to connect with the baby's mother. As we were leaving, she reached over and put a $5 bill into the child's hand. The mother was so surprised and visibly moved by this kind-hearted and generous stranger who was so lovingly and joyously gifting her child with money. This was just one of many instances when I witnessed Baba Nada's generosity. She was a selfless and willing giver, in every sense of the word.

I would often hear her say *"I am not afraid of dying, I could go today, and when my time comes, my only wish is that I go quickly rather than lose my dignity and become a burden on others."* Her wish was granted. Her faith in Source gave her what she had asked for. One day she woke up with a terrible headache that grew stronger. She called my father explaining that she wasn't well and that he needed to go over. When he arrived, he found my grandmother lying unconscious on the floor. Baba Nada died peacefully that night surrounded by her loved ones.

The discussions around gratitude, belief, and attracting abundance into your life have only recently become popular. A lot of people are talking about how gratitude has impacted and changed their life for the better. I guess I was fortunate. I had lived these through my Baba Nada, a woman who was wise beyond words— a true unconscious competent.

*"As we let our own light shine, we unconsciously give permission to other people to do the same.*

120

*As we are liberated from our own fear, our presence automatically liberates others."*

## The Baba Nada Let Your Inner Light Shine Reminders

*"Be good to others, and you will be good to yourself." - Nadezda Mihajlovic (Baba Nada)*

There was so much that all who knew Baba Nada had learned. She gifted many with her great wisdom and generosity. By living this way, she also brought herself some joy. The following are examples of how she lived and by adopting some of these strategies, you too will be able to inject more joy into your life.

### *Let Go of Your Mind and Live from Your Heart*

*"The intuitive mind is a sacred gift and the rational mind is a faithful servant. We have created a society that honors the servant and has forgotten the gift." - Einstein.*

My Baba Nada was a natural at living from her heart. I believe that this is why she was such a great negotiator. She did not let language barriers deter her heart's desires. She did not let fear get in her way. She connected through her heart. By the time she passed away, the entire shopping district on Smith Street in Collingwood, Melbourne, knew her. She left a mark. Because she allowed her heart to guide her, and to feel and connect with others without fear, she was able to bring out the light in others, like the beautiful Afghani refugee woman who had experienced the most difficult time. Baba Nada left a legacy that will go on for generations.

121

*"C'mon, that's a bit of a twist,"* I hear you say. *"I thought this book was about our minds and not our hearts."* You're right. But quieting the chatter in your mind and letting your heart guide you is important because it allows you to connect with your intuition.

Living through your heart means being guided by love, living with passion and desire, and eliciting the feeling of joy and excitement to be alive. We have purpose, and we have vision, and although we don't know how our heart's desire will be realized, we are excited knowing that that which we desire is being shaped and is right here, right now. We just need to open up and let it in.

Let's get even deeper here. Are you ready for the next twist? Well, what I have just said is evidence based. Science shows that there are neurotransmitters, ganglia, proteins, and support cells in the heart that are also found in the brain. According to extensive research conducted by the HeartMath Institute, this is true. This research indicates that our 'heart brain' acts independently of our cranial brain and has a large range of sensory capabilities.

Furthermore, there has been research on the stomach that indicates it shares the same neurons as the brain, and it also has an intuitive function. This means that we might have 2Minds, but we actually have three organs in our bodies that share an intelligence similar to the brain. Of course, the function of our brain is different from that of the heart and stomach, but when these three amazing minds work together in coherence, to guide each other, without the ego or the negative chatter taking over, we can use them to guide our dreams and desires. Our brilliant brain's function is to keep us alive through the thinking functions, through controlling the functions of our body, and through the fight or flight response. It allows us to process our day-to-day tasks, to retain beautiful memories, to compose and listen to music, to analyze and assess, to solve problems, to read a book, and on it goes, but you get the gist, right? Apart from the obvious biological functions of our heart and stomach, they are also able to sense and feel things that may not be explainable to the brain.

My father has always had an acute instinctive ability to know when my brother or I are in trouble, even when we are miles apart. Many years ago, my brother had a terrible car accident. Incredibly, my father knew that something dreadful was going to happen to one of us. He had had a dream the night before it happened and awoke with a strong feeling of dread in his stomach. A similar thing happened when I was ill on one occasion while living in Japan. I had just crawled back into bed having been bathroom bound for the last hour when the phone rang and there was my Dad asking me what was wrong. Japan is only two hours behind Australian Eastern Standard Time, and they had never called me so early in the morning. So, how do you explain my father's ability to know when the two most important people in his life are in trouble? Intuition. Intuition is real, and those neurons in the heart and stomach explain its function.

The emotions we feel and the state we are in internally radiates externally. We are made out of energy which radiates through strong currents from our body. The vibration of the heart radiates farther than the brain. According to the HeartMath Institute, our heart emits electromagnetic energy corresponding to our emotions, and this field, or the electromagnetic current from our heart, can be measured several feet away from our body. Moreover, the HeartMath Institute research also indicates that by feeling positive emotions we can increase the brain's capacity to make good decisions.

Your heart knows. But if you are not using your mind to work in coherence with the heart, your mind can undermine the direction in which

123

your heart is telling you to go. If you keep using your mind to ignore your heart, the voice of your heart softens to the point where you can barely hear it.

Your heart and gut contain thousands of neurons that can also be found in your brain.[2] Next time you have that 'gut feeling' or your heart is yearning to do something, listen to it. And then — take action!

Let's take this one step further. The stronger your emotions are, the stronger the vibration being emitted from your heart will be. Remember, it is now known that your heart radiates a powerful source of electromagnetic energy, and this energy can be felt outside of your body. We have all experienced this. You know that feeling of walking into a room, and you can sense the discomfort or tension in the air, only to find out that there had been an argument?

I guess the most important thing I want you to get out of this chapter is just how vital your intuition is. That 'gut feeling' you get about something is not just some irrational notion that should be dismissed. You now know that there is concrete evidence proving that what we call intuition is a result of neurons that are transmitted from our brains. They work together and rely on each other; however, if you let your brain and its perceived logic overpower the heart, you risk losing or weakening your intuitive ability. Listen to your gut. It's telling you something.

## *Express Your Emotions*

This book has gone into some detail about the wonderful and loving side of Baba Nada, but that is not to say she was just a sweet little old lady. I refer to her as a pocket rocket not only on account of her size, but on

---

2 For more information on the science based evidence related to the connection between our heart, brain, and gut and how they influence our emotions, intuition, and decision-making go to: https://www.heartmath.org/research/science-of-the-heart/

account of her strength and determination. Yes, Baba Nada was one hell of a loving, sweet woman, but she was also unafraid of expressing her emotions. When she was angry, you knew it. She would tell you how she felt, or her silence would show you, until she was ready to express it. Most of the time though, once she had said what she needed to say, she was done. She very rarely held grudges or rehashed old wounds.

She communicated how she was feeling. She trusted people, so she would speak to them about the hardships she suffered, particularly relating to her marriage and son. This allowed her to unburden herself but in a way that wasn't burdening to others. She had a way of drawing people in to listen and understand. And she returned the favor in spades with her ever willing ear and compassionate and understanding heart.

She was authentic and never faked her emotions. What you saw is what you got. She would cry when she was sad and grieve when she felt grief. She would speak about her loneliness, yet it was hard to imagine that she would feel lonely for long because of her ability to connect and attract people. Perhaps her ability to express her emotions was one of the reasons why she lived a full and healthy eight four years.

The message here shows the value of being genuine. Emotions are a part of being fully alive, and when we don't express them, we are prone to becoming mentally and physically ill. Express your emotions. Let them out. It is important, but don't allow the negative emotions to prevent you from living a full life. You are in control of your mind, so when life kicks you down, dust yourself off and get back up. Let it out, and then let it go. Move on, and always remember to give any person who has hurt you love. This may sound irrational and difficult, but letting go, moving on, and giving the other person love actually frees your mind of energy sapping grudges, negativity, and anger.

## *Express Gratitude and Appreciation Every Day*

Although Baba Nada relied on social security benefits, she was deeply grateful for what she considered to be her wealthy lifestyle. I never knew my grandmother to want for anything and if she did, she hid it well. She always seemed to have something to give. She gave us, her grandchildren, money whenever she saw us, she gave money to children she didn't know, and she lent money to anyone who asked her for it. And it was always repaid, as promised. If I needed some extra cash when I was growing up, Baba Nada was the one I went to. She willingly and lovingly gave to us. She never allowed her children or grandchildren to return the money that they had borrowed from her. She gave with joy.

Baba Nada was grateful for her perceived wealth, and apart from her una happy marriage, she was grateful for just about everything else too.

She felt that she lived like a queen. And a Queen she was. A Queen of people's hearts.

## *Live with Faith. Live with Conviction.*

Baba Nada was not one to pray or to strictly follow religious or traditional standards. She respected her culture, but she did not necessarily need to attend church every week to demonstrate the strength of her conviction. It was inside her, and her way of praying was through gratitude and talking to God in her own way. She did not just believe in God — she was convinced. Her conviction had survived the post WWII Communist regime of former Yugoslavia. Her faith was so strong that her external environment couldn't shake it, and as a result of this, somehow that external environment always improved.

Baba Nada dreamed of a better life, of living someplace where life was not only about survival. When she spoke about migrating to Australia, there was no doubt in her mind that it was her faith and conviction that led her and her family to the "lucky country", away from the hardships of the harsh peasant life in the Balkans.

I hear Bob Proctor talk about conviction all the time. He often references Napoleon Hill saying that if you want to realize something, you must first believe it will happen. If you do not believe, if you do not have faith, you are leaving yourself to sheer luck, chances are you will never realize your dream. There is a magic that comes through faith. It exerts confidence and strength, and it will show you the way. Baba Nada's conviction was evident through her actions. She never allowed fear to stop her because her faith and her conviction that things would work out were unwavering. If you know what you want and believe that you can achieve it, and then take action toward it, it will be yours to have. As the classic quote from Napoleon Hill claims, *"Whatever your mind can conceive and believe, it can achieve."*

## Have an Open Heart. Love Others.

*"Do to others as what you would have them do to you."*
*- Luke 6:31*

By living with an open heart and loving others, by seeing the best in people, and connecting with people, we lift our own and the other person's vibration. We are more likely to live in a state of coherence and unk consciously send that out into the world. It also means that our body is more likely to function in a state of coherence. This adds to our feeling of overall wellness and is important for our psychological and physical well-being. We are social beings and connecting at that deep level is a natural state. By connecting and seeing the best in others, we are more able to see the best in ourselves; we are more likely to experience joy and peace. By sharing someone else's joy, we increase our own.

I hope I have made clear by now that negative emotions such as resentment, jealousy, anger, control, and hatred do not serve us. In fact, they harm us more than they affect anybody else. These feelings do not only have a negative impact on your mind, but they also destroy peace of mind and can have a terrible impact on your psychological and physical health and wellbeing. It simply is not worth it.

Remember to feel it, let it out, and let it go. Forgive yourself first and foremost and forgive others. Why live burdened with emotional baggage? We cannot control other people's behavior. We only have control of our minds and our lives, so live lightly, live fully, and detach yourself from the heaviness of that unnecessary burden. Always remember what you give out must come back to you, and you simply don't need the crap. As Baba Nada would say, *"Look after and care for others, and God will look after you!"*

Baba Nada's open heart soothed. It uplifted, it connected, it laughed out loud with the other person (boy, she was fun!). It looked the person in the eye, and it connected with the deepest part of their soul. This is powerful because when you connect with the soul, you are connecting to innocence, purity, and perfection. You cannot connect with another person at a deep level by preaching what they should be, do, or have, or by trying to control them, by being resentful, hostile, and angry or dwelling on the wrongs of a person. When the soul speaks, it says that we are all one, we are perfect, and we are innocent because that is exactly what the soul is. There is no way that a person could not feel uplifted or not heard if you have truly connected to their soul. That is why people always felt important when they were around Baba Nada. She left them feeling so much better about themselves and about life.

The best thing about Baba Nada was she knew how to have fun. She enjoyed a little drink every now and then and had a wicked sense of humor. After all, what is life without fun and laughter? It brings us joy, and life is meant to be joyful.

## *Don't Be Afraid to Show Affection.*

In today's society, we have been bombarded by images that elicit fear. Neighbors are no longer talking, and we have developed a mistrust of anyone who may be different or who isn't in our inner circle. We are quick to judge and rarely practice stepping in another's shoes.

Baba Nada's warmth came not only from her light but also from her affection. So, to put it simply, live your life with the beauty of affection.

## *Have a Generous Spirit.*

*"Give and you shall receive." - Luke 6:38*

Give with an open and loving heart. Give because deep in your heart you want to give. Give because you already have everything. Give because through kindness and giving, you are creating a better world. Give because through genuine and loving giving, you too will receive love, joy, and generosity.

Give without expecting anything in return. However, remember to receive graciously when you are given to because you cannot truly give unless you are also open and willing to receive. The two are of the same principle really. What you give out will come back to you in abundance. As Bob Proctor would say *"Give generously and receive graciously."*

## *Be Your God Darn Self!!!*

Baba Nada was unique. She was comfortable in her own skin. She was sweet and generous with her love, yet her loud and passionate voice could be heard down the street. She was occasionally angry but never afraid of being vulnerable. She was old fashioned and traditional in some of her ways, but her wisdom exceeded tradition. Above all, Baba Nada was her God darn self. She never contemplated being anyone else. She was authentic, and that's where her strength came from. She never allowed her mind to tell her that she was not enough. Her mind was free from the anguish of having to be something that you are not.

We are all born unique, and there is beauty in our uniqueness. Yet somewhere we have picked up the message that we are not enough just as we are, so we mistakenly try to be something that we are not. We try to be liked, to fit in, to please others by hiding our authenticity. We have been hurt in the past, and we then carry this unnecessary hurt throughout our lives and those hurts lead us to believe that we are somehow not good enough.

Baba Nada's strength came from her lack of pretense. It's interesting that often we try to be someone else so that we are liked, yet when we do that, we lose the thing that makes us most interesting and beautiful to others — our uniqueness. This is where our real strength lies: our quirks, idiosyncrasies, and all that other stuff we are forever trying to change about ourselves. We are born perfect in our imperfection. Our uniqueness is what makes us attractive. It is where that light stems from. By hiding your true self just to be liked, you attract the wrong people and experiences to you.

Wouldn't it be easier just to relax and let your real self emerge in all its beauty and glory? Don't be afraid to do this. When you are able to relax and be you, life will complement you with ease and with an energy that attracts to you the quality of relationships, work, and life that you deserve. Respect will flow to you because you are in flow and brave enough to be you and nobody else. Besides all that, how much more fun and freeing would it be to let go of the burden of trying to be someone you're not? When your critical mind starts to try to take over and go back to its self-deprecating ways, gently tell it to move over because you ain't listening anymore. You now understand your true worth, and you're ready to let that light of yours shine bigger and brighter than ever.

# PART 3:

## Stepping Out Of Your Mind To Find Out Who You Truly Are

# Let Your Deepest Light Shine

*"Your playing small does not serve the world."*
*- Marianne Williamson*

I wanted to conclude this book with a similar message to the one at the beginning. I wanted the conclusion to leave you in the state of magnificence because it is critically important that you realize who you really are and that within you lies a well of glory and power beyond what you have ever imagined. The message fits nicely with the preamble and Bob Proctor's similar message to us about who you truly are.

This verse from Marianne Williamson's book *A Return to Love* so poignantly expresses who we truly are. It also shows the contrast of the 2Minds — one being fear driven, keeping us meek and feeling worthless, and the other being loving, reflecting the brilliance and perfection within each of us when we choose self love and embrace our perfectly imperfect truth. .

"Our deepest fear is not that we are inadequate,

Our deepest fear is that we are powerful beyond measure.

It is our light, not our darkness that most frightens us.

We ask ourselves, 'Who am I to be brilliant, gorgeous, talented, and fabulous?'

133

Who are you not to be? You are a child of God.

Your playing small does not serve the world.

There is nothing enlightened about shrinking so that other people won't feel insecure around you.

We are all meant to shine as children do.

We are born to make manifest the glory of God that is within us.

It is not just in some of us, it is in everyone.

As we let our own light shine, we unconsciously give permission to other people to do the same.

As we are liberated from our own fear,

Our presence automatically liberates others."

> - Marianne Williamson, *A Return to Love: Reflections on the Principals of A Course in Miracles.*

I discovered these precious words when I first read Marianne Williamson's book in 1994. They have stuck with me since then. I have them on the wall in my home as a reminder to myself, and to all who visit, of who we truly are. Even though they have been on my wall for many years, I have to look at them frequently to be reminded of that true essence residing in each and every one of us.

Ms. Williamson's words are unerringly eloquent and resonate deeply. Take the time to read and reread these words.

Examine them. As you read them, tap into your spirit, and your feelings. What are they telling you?

*"Our deepest fear is not that we are inadequate,*

*Our deepest fear is that we are powerful beyond measure*

*It is our light, not our darkness that most frightens us."*

Somewhere along the unique journey of our life, something begins to dim our sacred and natural light. Often, this starts to happen in childhood when we are bombarded with messages telling us to be humble, be quiet, to not ask for what we want and to just stop dreaming. Sometimes, these messages come from our parents. Sometimes, they are from teachers, or even other children. Many of us may have experienced traumatic events, such as abuse, family violence, illness, or bullying. Regardless what our experience in childhood was, whether it was positive or negative, most of us somehow end up growing up with our light needing to be buffered as it has dimmed but never completely extinguished.

Sadly, these messages continue to haunt us in adulthood. For women, they come in the form of constant media bombardment about how we should look and what we should be like, in order to reach society's standards of 'perfection'. We are assaulted with images of a beauty that has been so tweaked by Photoshop that it is beyond any realm of reality. And through this constant exposure to the unrealistic and unnatural ideals of beauty set by others, we forget our own. In fact, nobody can be more beautiful than anyone else, particularly when we let our inner light shine. We may all look different, but when we embrace our individuality through love and respect for ourselves, for others, and for life, we all become equally beautiful. It is our very uniqueness and diversity that make us so — no age, dress size, or eye color can take our true beauty away. Every single one of us is good enough, just as we are. We are infinite, exceptional, attractive, and worthy beyond measure. This is our deep, natural state.

The social constructs that lead to stereotypes only serve to instill false feelings of lacking something, in order to have control over us. They can

135

lead to feelings of unworthiness because, ultimately, we have forgotten who we truly are, and in doing so we have given them our power.

Women are not only bombarded with impossibly unattainable beauty ideals but also ideals about who we should be in the workforce, as people, and as mothers. Mothers are often placed in a box and judged. Sadly, these judgements and expectations often come from other women. Why do we do this to ourselves and to each other? I feel it can only come down to our own fear and insecurity.

Men are not free from this constant barrage either. Similar socially constructed ideals of masculinity are perpetuated, and the expectations of being 'a man' are, in many ways, as complex as those placed on women. Men are expected to be strong, assertive, and masculine, without displaying any signs of weakness. The expectations are as enormous as they are unrealistic.

It saddens me to think that many men and women feel unsafe or ashamed to be their unique selves. It is unfortunate that we live in a society where many feel they are not accepted the way that is natural to them. It is heartbreaking to think that a lot of people feel that they are not able to ask for help during difficult times because of the harsh judgement they may face.

I have battled with this for most of my life. Many times I would climb high — and some of my achievements were at quite a young age — only to tear myself down again through self-punishment and self-sabotage. Why punishment? Somehow, I felt guilty, unworthy, and ashamed for no other reason than the insanity of my mind. I allowed the other side of my mind to feed me these lies until I believed them, until they overtook and held the truth of who I really was hostage. It's interesting how the mind works when a message has been embedded in its subconscious. It is through these false thoughts and beliefs, these false paradigms in our subconscious minds, that we develop our self-image. Therefore, we continue to ask ourselves:

*"Who am I to be brilliant, gorgeous, talented, and fabulous?"*

And this is where Ms. Williamson challenges us by questioning:

*"Actually, who are you not to be? You are a child of God."*

No matter what your beliefs are around the concept of God, or if you even believe in God (whatever form God takes for you), each of us comes from the same Source, and, therefore, each of us carries within us the same essence, the same infinite potential, and infinite intelligence. Irrespective of where you were born, your upbringing, or your gender; if we were all created by the same Source, every single one of us has a light inside us that cannot be extinguished and that desperately wants to shine. It was meant to shine; that is its purpose.

Children are excited by the zest of life, their souls knowing that life is wonderful, and they embark on adventure, fun, and joy, with an instinctive and unquestioning faith. That is why they have such wonderful imaginations and dream about being great, about flying, dancing, performing, acting, and just living from their beautiful, joyful hearts, until it is taken away from them and they slowly start to forget who they truly are, and what their life's purpose is.

Read and reread Ms. Williamson's words until they penetrate deeply. Allowing yourself to give in to your deep, subconscious paradigms means not allowing your full potential and life purpose to be realized — not allowing joy to prevail. However, by really letting yourself and your deep inner light, joy, and your dream to grow, and by accepting your invaluable self-worth, you naturally allow that for those around you. How much better would the world be if every one of us was able to let go of our own false negative perceptions of who we are, to let go of our so-called limitations and let our true God-given nature shine? We all have a purpose and something that we were born to contribute to this world.

What would you do if you set yourself free from your own limitations?

How different would your life be?

And please remember:

*"Your playing small does not serve the world.*

*There is nothing enlightened about shrinking so that other people won't feel insecure around you.*

*We are all meant to shine as children do.*

*We are born to make manifest the glory of God that is within us.*

*It is not just in some of us, it is in everyone.*

*As we let our own light shine, we unconsciously give permission to other people to do the same.*

*As we are liberated from our own fear,*

*Our presence automatically liberates others."*

Thank you, Ms. Williamson, for these words, for the reminder, and for all that you have contributed to us through your teachings.

# Afterword — The Your2Minds Mission

*"Every living being is an engine to the wheel work of the universe. Though seemingly affected only by its immediate surrounding, the sphere of external influence extends to infinite distance." - Nikola Tesla*

When Bob Proctor spoke those mind-altering words, *"Did you know if you weren't here, the Universe would literally be out of alignment?"* my entire being was ready to hear them. It felt like the shackles of my mind had completely unlocked, and my soul had been set free to feel, to jump with joy, to be moved deeply, to show me who I truly was. The truth had been revealed. My soul had been unleashed, and I was thinking from deep within myself. I felt the true meaning of Bob's words that day.

We are all deeply connected to each other and to the Universe itself. We are all infinitely loved, important, and talented. Yet somewhere along the way, we forget this. You take one part away, and it is like taking a piece of the jigsaw puzzle away. It is never really complete. If we could just let go of that chatter in our mind and realize our own infinite and intrinsic value, we would allow ourselves to be in our natural state, and our natural state is pure love. It is greatness. It is genius.

If we allowed ourselves to see our own infinite value and to be guided by that, we would naturally come to know the piece of the Universal puzzle that we were put here to play. We would be guided by our soul's purpose rather than by our fear because fear is nothing to a being that has such a great purpose in the Universe. There is something that you were put here to do and accomplish, and nobody else alive has that same talent and ability. The piece of your puzzle is important. The whole puzzle cannot be completed without you.

Remember Marianne Williamson's words:

*"Your playing small does not serve the world.*

*There is nothing enlightened about shrinking so that other people won't feel insecure around you.*

*We are all meant to shine as children do.*

*We are born to make manifest the glory of God that is within us...."*

Just like you, I have my own infinite potential, my own piece of the puzzle that nobody else can match in quite the same way, and my piece is equally as important as everyone else's piece. I was meant to stand out. You too are meant to stand out. That is the only way we will ever properly serve others and serve life through our talents. Our shrinking, our fear, insecurity, and lack of self-confidence is not serving the world. It is not making the world a better place, by any means.

That day with Bob, my entire body was taken over by my soul. Everything finally seemed clear to me. I felt a big lump in my throat, but I held back my tears. I couldn't get emotional now. My mascara would run in front of Bob and the other consultants in that room, and I had the tendency to start bawling in the most inappropriate circumstances. I was sitting at the very front of the room where Bob was speaking. Can you imagine that scenario? This neurotic woman crying uncontrollably one meter away from the great Bob Proctor, black mascara running down her cheeks, her sobbing getting louder and interrupting Bob's important message...

Fortunately, with much effort, I managed to hold back my tears. I needed to stay focused on what was happening inside me. I cannot recall ever experiencing anything like it before. My soul had spoken, and boy, was it loud. It was clear that I had just had a strong message come through from Source. My body felt like it had fully and finally woken up. I was alert, and I was moved beyond words.

And then the message came through: "*You cannot go home being the same person. You simply cannot go home being the same person. You must write that book. It is time.*" As I told you earlier on, I had always dreamed of writing a book and had made a few attempts to do so in the past, but I never ended up completing them.

Completing a book was part of my plan, but I had planned to write it after I had established my business, had a family, and had the time to focus on writing. I have carried a vision, a deep desire to write since I was a child, but actually writing a book had been put under the list of things I would one day get to. There were other things that I needed to focus on first, before I could start writing again. Isn't it interesting how you put off your dream to do other things that appear to be more important at the time? Isn't it also interesting when you think you have a plan, and you know what will happen in that plan step by step? We try to hold on to our plans and insist that they must be executed in that perfect and exact way, but what I have learnt is we don't need to know the how. The steps will reveal themselves when you decide to do it and when you trust your intuition.

141

As soon as there was a tiny gap in the training I had been attending, I ran to Peggy McColl, who was sitting at the back of the room. I was compelled to talk to her. *"I need to talk to you. Will you be here all day?"* I asked her. I had to act as a matter of urgency. I had to show Source that I was ready to listen, to follow my intuition and guide, and, most importantly, I had to do this by acting immediately. I had to silence that negative chatter that told me I couldn't and that it wouldn't be good enough. It was time to get over that. I had to go home an author. I had to show myself that I was worthy of writing something of real value. I had to prove to myself that I was ready to have my dream become a reality.

I can't even remember what I said to Peggy when I approached her the second time. I tried to hold my tears back as I said something along the lines of *"I am in Canada for another week. I cannot go back to Melbourne the same person. I need to accomplish a dream. Do you think I could write a book in seven days?"* Peggy replied with one big and definite, *"YES!"* And the rest, as they say, is history.

I hope you find something relatable in my experiences and that you gain something from this book that is so dear to my heart. Most importantly, I hope that you will liberate your soul and allow it to shine as it is supposed to. You are magical, you are authentic, you are unique, and you are a very important piece of this epic puzzle that we call life. Go out and make a difference to yourself and to all who have the privilege to come into contact with you. It is your time, now.

CPSIA information can be obtained
at www.ICGtesting.com
Printed in the USA
LVHW040819280920
667265LV00004B/265

9 780648 857808